"There are other helpful books on _____, _____ much wisdom and heart as *Understanding Sexual Abuse* by Tim Hein. A survivor himself, Tim intersperses his own beautifully told story of healing throughout this extremely practical and biblical look at how to survive abuse and how to help those who've been abused. This book is a gift."

Michael Frost, Morling College, Sydney

"Only recently have survivors and Christian leaders had access to quality treatments of sexual abuse stories that do not hide from therapy or God! I felt like I was sitting in a safe place across from Tim, listening to his wisdom and sharing in a survivor's grief. *Understanding Sexual Abuse* is disarming in approach and creative in its mission. Here's a great tool to help struggling survivors in their healing journey."

Andrew J. Schmutzer, professor of Bible at Moody Bible Institute, author of *Naming Our Abuse: God's Pathways to Healing for Male Survivors of Sexual Abuse*

"Before this book was even finished I knew it must be written—that Tim's story needed to be told for it contains a powerful and needed witness. Written both from personal experience and with a pastoral touch, this is a healing, wise book for victims of sexual abuse, those who love them, and anyone leading in Christian churches or ministries today."

Mark Sayers, senior pastor of Red Church, Melbourne, Australia, author of *Disappearing Church* and *Strange Days*

"This book brings together Tim Hein's insights as a thoughtul educator, pastor, theologian, and survivor of child sexual abuse. This is a courageous book. Tim vulnerably shares his story of trauma and pain and his ongoing journey toward healing. He doesn't pretend to know exactly what other survivors have experienced but instead offers his insights in ways that show understanding of the multiple impacts of abuse on survivors and offer pathways of support and healing. Survivors of abuse will find sources of healing and hope in this resource. This book is a gift to people engaged in Christian ministry. Tim draws from trauma research and biblical, theological, and pastoral foundations to equip Christian ministers to offer compassionate, careful, and well-informed support to survivors."

Deidre Palmer, senior lecturer in Christian education, family and children ministries, Adelaide College of Divinity

UNDERSTANDING
SEXUAL
ABUSE

A GUIDE FOR
MINISTRY LEADERS
AND
SURVIVORS

TIM HEIN
FOREWORD BY DEBRA HIRSCH

IVP Books
An imprint of InterVarsity Press
Downers Grove, Illinois

InterVarsity Press
P.O. Box 1400, Downers Grove, IL 60515-1426
ivpress.com
email@ivpress.com

InterVarsity Press® is the book-publishing division of InterVarsity Christian Fellowship/USA®, a movement
of students and faculty active on campus at hundreds of universities, colleges, and schools of nursing in the
United States of America, and a member movement of the International Fellowship of Evangelical Students.
For information about local and regional activities, visit intervarsity.org.

Scripture quotations, unless otherwise noted, are from the New Revised Standard Version of the Bible,
copyright 1989 by the Division of Christian Education of the National Council of the Churches of Christ in
the USA. Used by permission. All rights reserved.

Content in chapter 4 from pages 56–57 of The Courage to Heal: A Guide for Women Survivors of Child
Sexual Abuse, *third edition, revised and updated, by Ellen Bass and Laura Davis. Copyright © 1994 by*
Ellen Bass and Laura S. Davis Trust. Reprinted by permission of HarperCollins Publishers.

While any stories in this book are true, some names and identifying information may have been changed to
protect the privacy of individuals.

Cover design: David Fassett
Interior design: Daniel van Loon
Cover image: water droplet background: © Maslovpapa/iStockphoto
watercolor background: © larisa_zorina/iStockphoto

ISBN 978-0-8308-4135-6 (print)
ISBN 978-0-8308-8104-8 (digital)

Printed in the United States of America ∞

InterVarsity Press is committed to ecological stewardship and to the conservation of natural resources in all our
operations. This book was printed using sustainably sourced paper.

Library of Congress Cataloging-in-Publication Data
A catalog record for this book is available from the Library of Congress.

P	21	20	19	18	17	16	15	14	13	12	11	10	9	8	7	6	5	4	3	2	1
Y	35	34	33	32	31	30	29	28	27	26	25	24	23	22	21	20	19	18			

To Priscilla

CONTENTS

FOREWORD

Debra Hirsch

This book is a courageous gift, arriving at just the right time.

Our entire culture, including our churches, is only beginning to come to grips with the vast and insidious topic of sexual abuse. The sheer scale of the issue is hard to fathom.

But we must. No Christian leader can answer the call of ministry today and not be informed about this issue. Despite the complexity, we must engage. Similarly, survivors also deserve answers that go to the heart of their pain, naming the issues, engaging their hard questions, offering full and frank information, and carefully proclaiming the vastness of God's love to empower them for the road toward recovery.

This powerful book meets both these needs. It is a book every survivor deserves, and that every Christian leader needs to read.

Tim Hein has been a friend for over fifteen years, but I don't need to be biased to affirm the power and beauty of this book. Rather, knowing Tim and observing his life and ministry only confirms my confidence in the integrity of this story. It is no surprise that he has written such an eloquent and moving resource, filled with precise explanations and rich insight.

Tim is a person after my own heart, passionate about seeing the church as a radical community of people walking toward wholeness and welcoming broken people—a place where the radical gospel of Jesus Christ is announced as good news, even in the darkest places and in the face of the most difficult issues in our world. We follow a God who is also a trauma survivor, a God who endured the cross. Tim captures this rugged truth about our God, and offers a genuine, eloquent explanation of what it means to walk unafraid through the storm of trauma.

Drawing courageously from his own experiences as both a survivor and a Christian leader, Tim's careful research is complemented by an empathy drawn from the ache of his own experience. It is deeply sensitive, and yet never gets bogged down in sentiment. It is a constructive book, navigating the issue with clarity. It is a strong book, courageously unpacking the various elements of complex trauma, and then delving into the big questions of suffering. And, despite the difficult subject, it is a safe book—an essential pastoral resource.

I must mention the beautiful Priscilla too, because her experiences of pain and recovery are included, a testimony to her courage. Tim and Priscilla live with a passion for God's redemption of our world, and this book is sure to be a genuine contribution to the recovery of many.

Tim has given us a readable, useful, and passionate guide to this most intimidating of topics. It is a gift of a book, essential reading for survivors, no matter their stage of recovery. It's also essential for every Christian leader, not only to read themselves but to keep close at hand to give to others when the pastoral moment arrives.

INTRODUCTION

It is said that the true test of a society is how it treats its most vulnerable members.

In our society today, it is estimated that up to one in four girls and one in six boys experience sexual abuse during childhood. Experts also estimate that as many as half of the incidents are not reported. Millions of people, both children and adults, face each day with this hidden, complex pain. Leaders and loved ones struggle to understand their experience.

I have experienced this personally; I was sexually abused as a child. I've written this book to inform fellow victims and to help them become survivors. But I'm also an ordained minister, and I want to inform other leaders about this issue. Therefore, what I share is drawn not only from research but also from my experience as a survivor of sexual abuse and as a Christian leader who has assisted others on this journey. Christian leaders live on the front line of ministry with hurting people. It is crucial that we are informed and equipped to respond to the complexity of this issue. I hope this book can be a useful guide to the nature and trauma of child sexual abuse for both survivors and ministry leaders.

I also know this journey from the perspective of being the partner of a survivor. My wife, Priscilla, suffered the abuse of her father. She generously shares portions of her story in this book, as well as insights from her knowledge and experience. She is also now an ordained minister.

To be clear, this is not a book about how to prevent abuse or how to deal with perpetrators. I write as a survivor and as a Christian leader, not as a psychologist or a therapist. It's a book geared for church and ministry leaders, to prepare them to support survivors of sexual abuse, and it also includes content specifically geared for survivors. It can be read by both kinds of readers. You will see that often I write as "we" throughout the book. By that I mean you and me—we the survivors, and we the Christian leaders. Those two perspectives, as well as careful research, have informed the insights that follow.

Defining Sexual Abuse

The term *sexual abuse* can cover a range of acts, but it most specifically refers to undesired sexual behavior of one person upon another. In this book, we're exploring the subject of *child sexual abuse*, and in that case there is really no need for the word *undesired* in the definition. Any sexual behavior by a person toward a child, that is, a person under the legal age of consent, is abusive. *Pedophilia* is an abnormal or perverted attraction to children. The legal term is *molestation*, which technically means "to disturb or interfere with." It is the use of a child, directly or indirectly, as a sexual object. None of the terms feel quite adequate, and of course unwanted sexual behavior is traumatic at any age. So while this book focuses specifically on child sexual abuse, many of the principles in these pages may apply to a variety of sexual assaults.

But let me be clear: If you have experienced abuse, I can't pretend to completely know you. People respond to abuse and trauma in different ways. You may resonate with some things in this book, and not others. That's okay.

I know *my* experience, and I know it was hell. I also know something of Priscilla's experience from the perspective of our close relationship. On the occasions when I have shared my insight with others, they have resonated with it. But I don't want to pretend to know yours. I say this to respect that you may be experiencing deep pain even as you read this, and I want you to know that you're not alone. I hope that what you find in the pages that follow speaks truth and helps you. There is a way forward.

If you are a Christian leader, this issue may seem baffling, ugly, and frightening. I hope sharing my story here and these key principles will also give you confidence to walk unafraid into the mess of ministry in a safe and informed manner.

This is not a therapeutic book, because I am not a psychologist or trauma expert. It's designed to give you knowledge, because knowledge is power, and recovery begins with empowerment. And that's why I believe my story, with glimpses of Priscilla's story as well, may be helpful. Our perspectives as survivors and ministry leaders have given us insights that I think are truthful and useful. In the pages that follow, I explore the questions that I wanted answered, both as a survivor and as a Christian leader. I try to carefully and clearly unpack this dark and mysterious subject and offer you a map.

Before I Share My Story

I'm aware of how difficult it can be to hear about someone else's story of abuse. But I also know how helpful it is to learn about someone else's experience. It's fine line, so I want to dispel one fear and one myth right from the start.

First, I'm not going to go into the specific details of our actual abuse experiences. You don't have to be afraid that you'll turn a page and suddenly be confronted by vivid details. The purpose of this book is to empower and inform, not to shock you. I share about my feelings and the facts of my life journey, but nothing more. You are safe in that regard.

Second, I want to dispel a myth that many victims of abuse spin constantly around in our minds: namely, that "What happened to me probably wasn't as bad as what happened to them." Sometimes we feel that we are not worthy of the attention and care that our pain desperately requires, compared to the horrible things we hear from other victims. That's another reason I'm not sharing the specific details of our experiences. Trying to compare painful experiences is a profound mistake. We rarely really understand other peoples' experiences, and we can never make a true comparison. Pain is not a measurable quantity, and child sexual abuse is traumatic for complex reasons. Most importantly, when we compare ourselves with others in this area, we have a tendency to dangerously downplay our experience before we fully comprehend it. We are guided by the myth that ignoring, downplaying, or denying our memories will minimize them and help us control them.

Survivors and Christian leaders both need to hear this clearly: every incident of abuse is traumatic. Downplaying our abuse almost always adds to our trauma. Priscilla and I offer our stories here not as special examples, or for any comparison; indeed, the sad reality is that they are not unique. We share our stories to show why abuse is so deeply destructive, and to explain how recovery can be possible. Child sexual abuse happens.

It happened to me, it happened to Priscilla, it may have happened to you, and it is horrific every single time.

The Church and Abuse by Clergy

It's important to name up front the failures of many churches in this area. Child abuse occurs right across society, including in churches and Christian organizations. Perpetrators have at times been Christian leaders, including ordained clergy. It is hard to find the words to sufficiently condemn this horrific behavior. That church denominations have not been further ahead of the procedural curve in systemically mitigating against this is deeply regrettable. But in those instances where it has been ignored, minimized, or even covered up, they have demonstrated a complicity that is difficult to imagine. It is hard to think of a more antithetical activity to the gospel of Jesus Christ than child abuse.

But child sexual abuse occurs right across society, in families and among trusted family friends, as well as in schools and other community organizations. I was abused by a male babysitter; Priscilla was abused by her father. As a society, we are just coming to grips with the proximity and prevalence of this issue.

I hope and pray this book not only helps empower survivors in their journey of recovery and healing but also gives Christian leaders confidence to face the reality of the issue and to enable recovery in any way they can.

My Story Begins

Growing up in Traralgon, a city in the Victoria region of Australia, was not unlike growing up in Springfield, the fictitious home of

The Simpsons. It's a medium-sized regional town surrounded by that strange combination of dairy farms and power stations.

I had a reasonably normal 1980s childhood: apart from school and organ lessons, I spent my time riding my BMX, watching *Knight Rider*, playing Australian Rules football, collecting Star Wars figures, and listening to Petra and Bon Jovi. My family attended a Pentecostal church that met in a high school hall in the next town.

Both of my parents were always around, and busy and productive in the community. Our home was full of church friends and laughter. It was my parents' natural hospitality that led to them open our home to Greg, the son of friends some distance out of town. Greg had obtained a job at a local store and needed a place to board during the week. Our caravan in the backyard was an ideal option.

It was exciting to have Greg live with us. He liked to joke around and rode a motorbike. It was also a blessing for my parents, who now had a live-in babysitter. Every second Wednesday evening was our church's prayer meeting, which previously meant I had to spend many hours sleeping on the floor at church. Now, with Greg there to babysit, a normal bedtime was possible.

I was nine years old, and 7:00 p.m. was my bedtime, with some leeway time for reading. But as is typical for a child, after the lights go out, time slows down. This defining time, before I fell asleep, was a time of serious and varied thinking. I digested the events of the day, let my imagination run loose, and turned future hopes into plans and wishes into longings.

As every child knows, with so much time staring at the ceiling, waiting for sleep, any interruption is welcome. So it was initially a pleasant surprise when Greg started popping into my bedroom to visit.

But in those visits, Greg abused me.

Where My Story Leads

I didn't disclose my abuse to anyone until I was in my early twenties. I carried the dark secret alone all those years before I told anyone at all, and did not finally tell my parents until a decade after that, when I was in my thirties. Over those years, what appeared to be normal life on the surface was marked for me by flashbacks, nightmares, and lonely anguish.

What made this process more complex was a deep personal sense that I was obligated to immediately forgive Greg for what he had done. This became a private mountain for me to conquer. In my young mind I thought that to be a good Christian I had to forgive him, and this burden set up a trajectory of stress and intense pressure, the effects of which I still sometimes experience today. It also led me to seek out and meet Greg in person. I promised him I wouldn't tell the police, preferring to keep the weight of my experience to myself. I thought I was doing the righteous thing.

Several years later, through counseling and the pastoral skill of a Christian leader named Bob, I was finally freed to unlock the traumatic door, release the truth, and begin to discover the experience of walking unafraid. This led to the filing of charges, Greg's conviction, and a strange encounter with the judge in court I did not expect. It also led to more searching, counseling and therapy, questions, anger, fear, reading, tears, and prayer. It led me further along a difficult journey that I can only describe in hindsight as a slow, deep, unwinding release.

ONE

A SAFE PLACE

*The truth does not change according to our
ability to stomach it emotionally.*

FLANNERY O'CONNOR

Then you will know the truth, and the truth will set you free.

JOHN 8:32 (NIV)

TIM'S STORY

The exact moment I realized I'd been sexually abused as a child, my family and I were waiting at an intersection in our car. We were on our way to lunch after church. I was fourteen years old.

I wasn't trying to think about it, and no one had mentioned it. It just came to me. I remember looking out the side window, zoning in on the raindrops dribbling down the window just in front of my face. This long moment remains like a still photo in my memory. My mind scanned my memory back and forth, recognizing, confirming. That happened to me. I've been abused.

As the car began to move forward, I tried to come to grips with this new information. I felt nervous and overwhelmed in my seat. A huge weight seemed to press into my chest, close to my throat. I undid my seatbelt and looked around the backseat.

> My parents were talking to each other in the front seats, oblivious. To say anything to them was unthinkable. My nervousness shifted to fear, to an almost sick feeling. As the car drove on, I watched the passing houses and shops, sitting with this new truth, so suddenly and unavoidably present.
>
> My young brain had somehow realized, comprehended, this uninvited truth. It would be a long time before I could find the proper words to describe the strange feeling of the painful memories. The closest I can come is that it felt like a shocking, overwhelming sadness. But it was more than sadness. I was unsettled, uncomfortable, and anxious.
>
> As the car drove on, I didn't move in my seat, and I didn't speak a word about it. I wouldn't for another eight years.

Your church is not an exception. There are victims of sexual abuse in every community and institution in society, including churches. There are certainly victims of sexual abuse in your congregation. One of the serious dilemmas of the subject of child sexual abuse is that while it is incredibly widespread, it is also shrouded in secrecy and even denial. It is often invisible in our congregations because of the silence of the victims themselves. Powerful forces can keep it so, and the shame that victims feel can perpetuate the idea that "good" families are exempt from its reach.

But the now significant body of research agrees that sexual abuse spans races, socioeconomic classes, and religious and ethnic groups. Investigations clearly indicate that churches are no exception. Much media attention has focused on the Catholic Church, because of the significant number of clergy who have been found to be perpetrators. I believe we may yet see the full extent of the disclosures elsewhere.

The specific issue of guarding against pedophilia in churches is outside the scope of this book. Even aside from the specific topic of abuse by clergy, we must not be blind to the fact that all church communities can be targets for pedophiles. It is absolutely essential that stringent policies and procedures be implemented in every ministry context, in line with standards set by state authorities and denominational bodies.

Our focus is on cultivating a safe church, where victims can become survivors. For this to occur, we must grasp clearly the fact that many in our congregations suffer in silence. Sadly, I am no longer surprised by who turns out to be a survivor. They are our neighbors, our friends, our colleagues, and certainly our congregation members.

This may seem a rather pedantic point to make to someone who has already decided to read this book. But I risk sounding pedantic for the purpose of clarity: too many people have ignored the issue of sexual abuse. We are beholden to look honestly at this uncomfortable reality, to accept the responsibility that comes with serving a community in a world where this evil occurs, and to be ready and able to respond to that reality. This begins with the clear decision that our church will be a safe place, well informed on the issue of sexual abuse.

Sermons Can Be Triggers

There's a powerful dynamic at work when a speaker stands before a group of people, particularly when that speaker is sharing the Word of God. But consider that in any congregation, a number of people will have experienced sexual abuse in childhood. Just acknowledging that fact helps us recognize the profound responsibility we have. The words we use in sermons can trigger unwanted images, feelings, and memories for these people.

Triggers are words and actions that prompt memories we would not have otherwise. We all experience triggers every day. Consider how hearing an old song, or a certain smell, can immediately take us back to a situation from years before. We may recall a long-buried memory that suddenly becomes vivid. Most of the time these moments are enjoyably nostalgic.

For abuse survivors, however, triggers can prompt flashbacks of the abuse experience or the feelings associated with the trauma. These experiences may continue throughout survivors' entire lives: I experience triggers to this day. Whenever I hear the name of the man who abused me, it has an effect on me unlike any other name. It is directly associated with the abuse. Whenever the topic of sexual abuse comes up on the radio or television, it captures not only my ear but also my mind's eye and my emotions. I'm also triggered when I see a certain type of pleated pants that Greg wore.

We cannot control these instances—they occur inevitably. I can't control it if someone named Greg stands before me wearing pleated pants. But I do know that this experience would have a strong emotional effect on me. The first thing on my mind would not be what they were talking about. We'll discuss how survivors can have strategies to manage triggers in a later chapter, but my point here is that Christian leaders should be conscious that at all times we are potentially speaking to some deeply vulnerable people.

Many people have been abused but have not disclosed their abuse to anyone. So we need to be aware that there may be a sizable number of individuals in our churches with unprocessed trauma. We must be careful how we speak, especially during a worship service. This is a place where people are willingly open and vulnerable, singing profound declarations of worship and seeking to receive teaching about matters related to their core values. It's a precious place.

Christian leaders should avoid making spontaneous comments about abuse. If we are going to address the topic of sexual abuse from the pulpit, through preaching, testimony, or teaching on the subject by an expert or a survivor, be sure to let the congregation know beforehand. Remember, it's not our role to try and trigger memories to evoke a response from people. A public worship gathering is not a safe context for this kind of deep, personal ministry. It requires private, professional focus and care.

Of course, we can't constantly walk on eggshells, afraid of how everything we say might play out in each and every life. We can and will inevitably trigger memories for people through our ministry. The next chapter will deal with how to respond when someone does actually disclose their experience of sexual abuse to us. But we must always be prudent and pastorally sensitive to the fragility of some members of our congregations.

Of course sermons can also be empowering and transformative, as the good news of the gospel is proclaimed to our hearts. Too many times to count I have been encouraged and equipped by faithful preaching. Often the sermon will be the only Christian word a suffering person receives, and it can be a defining moment in their life.

I suggest that we regularly say toward the end of our services, "If anything that's been said has touched on or triggered something for which you'd like prayer or counsel, be aware we have these people available to speak with." I know one church that not only has people available after the service but also includes a contact number in their bulletin that people can call and request to speak with someone during the week. This may seem obvious, but part of being a safe church is making the obvious explicit.

Understand the Subtle Power of Leaders

If we want a safe and informed church, then as Christian leaders we must also come to appreciate the subtle power we hold in our church community due to our position. Because personal behavior so strongly influences the culture of the church community, people intuitively look to the church's leaders as a barometer of expected behavior. Our words and actions signal what our community's standard is. If we want a safe church, we must be safe leaders. Do we model the personality traits of a community conducive to helping people feel safe and welcome? Or are we trying to impress, and thus increasing the distance to others?

Leaders can demonstrate this principle through small details. For example, rather than being the hero of our own sermon illustrations, we can use examples when we were the student in a situation, rather than the teacher. We can demonstrate humility by honestly confessing our faults and owning our mistakes, and praising those who corrected us. Consider how we respond and speak to children. Do we just glance down at them, or do we take the time to squat down to their level? What about the volume of our voice or the language we use?

We should also be careful to avoid even slightly sexist jokes, and always respect people's personal space, taking the time to ask someone's permission before shutting the door of our office. These small habits send messages, and I'd encourage us all to consider how we can identify and modify these small details so that our lives engender the trust required for a vulnerable person to feel safe in our presence.

Let me give you another example. In meetings, many male leaders instinctively slump low in their chairs, with their legs slightly apart, and pushed forward. Despite the fact that it's poor posture, I know this can be a temptingly comfortable way to sit. But as a female leader once pointed out to me, this posture means we are prominently displaying our groin to the group. We don't think about it consciously, but women can notice it. It sends a subtle and impolite message of carelessness regarding personal boundaries. The same is true when we lean too closely over someone or step in too close when we speak with them. This is an issue not just for male leaders but for female leaders too. We should take thoughtful care with our speech, manner, and dress to communicate that this is a community that respects and cares for everyone. Rather than dressing to impress, dress to appear approachable.

Someone once told me that I had a habit of walking quickly, looking down, through the foyer of the church I was a pastor in at the time. I am an introvert, and I generally have several matters brewing in my mind simultaneously. But I was told it conveyed that I was in a rush, with important things to do—more important than relating to everyday people. What an indictment! That's the opposite of how I feel. I could protest my innocence, but my actions had communicated a particular attitude to my congregation.

A pastor friend of mine was so determined to understand the gender dynamics of his ministry that he invited a female leader from the denomination to teach him the history of women's experience in that church. We cannot brush over these matters as we explore the weightier issues in future chapters. As leaders, our cues can be the defining difference in creating a safe culture in our church.

Train and Communicate

We need to take the time to train our leaders not only in leadership or evangelism but also on the topic of sexual abuse. I believe we should include teaching and training on sexual abuse for all our leaders, including volunteers. It's important that they have some basic knowledge of this complex subject and clear understanding of the principles of child protection and expected procedures of response. When the church conducts this kind of training, it communicates that it is unafraid to tackle this topic and sends a powerful message that the church takes seriously its responsibility to create a safe environment for those who are broken and hurting.

We can reinforce this value by making sure there's information on our church website or in newsletters and posters about available counseling services. In as many ways as possible, cultivate a culture of safety. Remember, a church is a community where people come not only with particular brokenness but also *to be vulnerable*. The mysterious dynamics of singing, worship, prayer, preaching, and fellowship create an atmosphere where people's innermost feelings and values are opened, challenged, healed, and nurtured. There really is nothing quite like being a part of a safe and informed local church.

Don't Go Hunting for Trauma

It's not our role to try and coax the disclosure of a survivor. We must be very careful about this. These matters touch survivors' deepest wounds. Being in control of the moment of disclosure is actually an important part of a survivor's ultimate healing. When people are ready, they will share.

The church leader's task is to cultivate an environment where people feel safe. Especially in regard to sexual abuse, we want people to know that this is a place that will support and empower them, whatever they decide to do. We should never try to take that step for them, whether through altar calls, prophecies, sermons, or counseling. We should never try to manipulate or push someone to disclose.

In the following chapters we'll deal specifically with how to understand and help people who disclose childhood experiences of sexual abuse. Responding appropriately requires a determination to cultivate a church community that is trustworthy, safe, and informed. And this begins in the heart of the Christian leader.

Finding the Safety to Reveal Abuse

Realizing that you were sexually abused as a child is a profoundly scary experience. While many survivors have always been aware, for some it is a gradual realization that becomes clearer as they grow older. Then, either as they reach an age of understanding or through a particular triggering event, one day it clicks.

That was Priscilla's experience. I did not see Greg for several years after my abuse, but she saw her father every single day. She recalls having a constant fear and sick feeling around him as she grew older, but it never added up to a cognitive realization of what was happening to her until she was watching a television show one day. The storyline involved a child disclosing abuse. She immediately realized what had been happening to her over the years, and it prompted her to disclose to her boyfriend, and soon after to her mother.

But experiences are varied. Many can hardly recall a day when they've not had to face these memories. This may be because the abuse occurred at (or continued into) a later age. But if the experience occurred in preteen childhood, flashes of memory accompanied by ugly feelings can make the horrible truth increasingly more vivid until they reach an age where they cross a line into conscious comprehension. Generally this occurs once they're old enough to understand more about what sexual abuse actually is. They learn about it on television, at school, or from their parents. It may take some time as their minds link the newfound knowledge with their unconscious memories, until suddenly the past pushes to the front of their mind. For both Priscilla and I, this happened in our teens. Others, however, don't realize what has happened to them until they are well into adulthood.

I have no idea what triggered my thoughts that day in my parent's car. They just suddenly turned to the topic of sexual abuse, and I realized that I had experienced it. But does that mean I had *forgotten* about it? Well, yes, you could put it that way. For a time the abuse had not been at the front of my mind.

I had blocked it out, buried it—waiting for the time when something would uncover or trigger it. It was waiting for me to grow old enough to understand. I was discovering a fact about myself, and that fact had a name: child sexual abuse.

Some survivors feel guilty about not realizing sooner, as if they've minimized the act. But this is beyond our control. I was a young teenager when I understood what had happened, and at that stage childhood memories come in moments, like photos, not like a film. I'd not thought about it prior to that morning. It had been filed with so many other childhood memories, present but unrecognized. When my mind put the pieces together that day, it suddenly made sense. I knew it was true.

Some survivors never forget, and live with vivid images and painful memories throughout their childhood. Others have unpleasant inklings but try to ignore them and never allow their minds to stop and reflect deeply on them. For still others, this takes many years, and they don't face the past until well into adulthood. It may seem quite a strange example, but I resonate with that scene in *Return of the Jedi* when Luke Skywalker reveals to Princess Leia that she is actually his sister. She is shocked, and yet she replies, "Somehow, I've always known."

Many survivors experience something akin to shock when they realize that something so traumatic has happened to them. This is called delayed recall, or posttraumatic amnesia. It is common in cases of sexual abuse, especially when the abuse occurred for a defined period of time and then stopped while the survivor was still a child. We rarely recall memories before the age of three, and have very limited memory up to the age of ten. My earliest memory is of the fish markets in Enschede, Holland, where we stayed for a several months when I was four. The images are fleeting but present in my mind's eye, as are the smells.

So while we carry a huge array of memories from childhood, we forget an incredible amount, too. Consider all the data our senses receive every day. Over the years we can't possibly consciously hold on to all of it, and yet our brains seem to organize it somehow, identifying patterns and holding onto data reinforced through repetition. The experience of delayed recall, or post-traumatic amnesia, is a kind of protective mechanism our brains use because we are unable to comprehend the reality and extent of the trauma, especially when we're young. As children, we may not have the mental or emotional capacity to recognize that what was happening to us was abusive. That does not mean that we were indifferent to it: indeed, it may have involved physical pain, or we may have wanted it to stop, or even hated it.

But psychologists affirm that in cases of extreme emotional trauma in children, our ability to consciously consider what has occurred may be delayed until we have the ability to understand it or put our feeling into words. In my experience, I suddenly became consciously aware that *abuse* was something I had experienced. I reached a moment when my mind turned itself to the subject. It came into the front of my thoughts. I suddenly *knew* it.

For some people this moment of realization occurs in therapy. They may have gone for reasons related to the effects of abuse, and the safe context in which they carefully processed their thoughts and memories led to recalling the traumatic or abusive event from years before. We all tend to remember more when we're prompted or "triggered" by something familiar, such as an old photo or a memento from school. Suddenly images flood back: people, names, peculiar details, even smells. Watching a home movie or browsing through a family photo album can do it. Stories can do it, too, when we hear anecdotes from friends that suddenly remind us of other situations, people, and events. Some feelings of nostalgia are very strong, almost like reliving snapshots of the past.

But sometimes the lapse of time and the distance in age and maturity give us a new perspective on an old memory. Thinking back as an adult, we suddenly realize a truth that we didn't see as a child, even though it is so familiar. Suddenly we see what we never saw before, and it all makes sense. For many of us, a similar process occurs at the moment we became aware of past abuse. Sometimes we never forget at all, sometimes the knowledge arrives with a growing awareness—and sometimes it explodes like a bomb.

Facing the Truth

At this point, some survivors begin to wonder if it would have been better if they'd never remembered anything. That same part of us will be tempted to brush the memories aside, or try to forget them, pushing them down and covering them over. But not being consciously aware of abuse doesn't mean we're immune to its effects. It doesn't mean the experience hasn't been traumatic. We will explore this dynamic later on, but for now I urge you, as someone who has walked this path myself, not to try to deny the difficult truth when it appears. This is a frustrating, dangerous, and ultimately impossible feat.

Many thoughts will rush around our minds at this time: questions, fears, and even some doubts. One significant doubt we often have is whether it really happened at all. I have sat with several people who confessed their fear that they may have just invented it somehow. *What kind of horrible person would I be if I were making all this up?* they wonder.

We worry that no one will believe us. In a sense it feels like the entire story exists only in our memory—in our head—so how do we know it's true? Our mind wanders into this kind of doubt because we are struggling to comprehend the enormity of the experience. It seems too enormous to be true. Doubting is a perfectly normal way of coming to grips with shocking news.

We might also think about how the person often seems such an unlikely perpetrator. How could he or she have committed these horrible acts? Most people picture sexual predators as strangers, anonymous people preying on playgrounds or abducting children off the street. But this image of sexual abuse is by far the less frequent, even if those are the stories that get broadcast on the news.

The truth is that eight out of ten survivors know their abuser. For both Priscilla and me, the perpetrator was actually living in our house. The overwhelming majority of perpetrators are trusted friends, family members, or neighbors. They are the people no one suspects. It's important to know this so that you do not feel like your experience is somehow unlikely or doubtful just because it happened somewhere familiar or was perpetrated by someone familiar.

You may think about how friendly, loved, or popular the person is who committed the act. Or how powerful they are, as figures of authority in your family or community. They don't seem like the kind of person who would do this, and you are the only one who knows what they've done.

Somehow it can feel more likely that we've imagined something than that this person really committed a true, verifiable act. This is an especially likely thought if the abuse occurred a long time ago. Is it just a fragment of my imagination?

We are not going to be able to cope with our realization by ourselves. We need help and support even to comprehend the enormity of what we are realizing. Studies suggest that more than half of sexual abuse incidents are not disclosed. There are too many people who don't get past the point of their private realizations, and struggle alone.

A Defining Moment

Sexual abuse shapes our feelings, fears, instincts, and even our personalities throughout childhood. In this most vulnerable of life stages, our inner world is undermined. This is why the moment when we realize and acknowledge to ourselves that we've been abused is a profoundly important one. And though it is a horrible experience to remember, it's also a defining moment, and it contains a strange element of hope.

Why? Because it marks the point when we begin to take back our life. In that moment, then and there, it is devastating news. It is almost too horrible to comprehend. But it brings to light something that has long been pulling the strings in the recesses of our mind for some time. Now we see at least that there is a situation, a problem—a reason for our struggles all along. Ultimately, the words of Princess Leia will resonate: somehow, we have always known. The pain from our memory now shouts its presence. This is just the beginning of the journey—but remember, we are only in chapter one. This moment is about recognizing the truth: the moment I can say to myself, *this happened.*

TWO

WHY ABUSE HURTS

On and on the rain will fall, like tears from a star,
On and on the rain will say how fragile we are.

STING, "FRAGILE"

Take care that you do not despise one of these
little ones; for, I tell you, in heaven their angels
continually see the face of my Father in heaven.

MATTHEW 18:10

PRISCILLA'S STORY

I am a teenager, lying on my bed, reading a magazine after school. Suddenly a flashback image appears of my father on top of me, so vivid that I can feel him. The image repeats like a video loop. I am trapped, and I find it hard to breathe. I'm in absolute suffocating terror.

These flashbacks are a regular occurrence for me. I don't have the mental strength to block them or to think about something else. I jump off the bed and run downstairs and outside, down to the nearby beach. I want to scream in someone's face. Just once, I want to be able to make someone understand what I feel, what it's like to be me. But I don't know how to do that, and strangely,

I don't know if that is allowed. I am the kind of teenage girl who always does the right thing.

Adrenaline seethes through my veins, and I take off down the beach, running as fast as I can, on and on, desperate for exhaustion to blunt my feelings. Finally, I collapse on the sand and wail, crying and screaming into the dusk, "It's not fair! It's not fair!"

I wonder how I'll ever survive a lifetime of this. The fear is relentless—not just that someone might do it again, but that I will have to spend my life reliving these memories. What is the future even for? I know that I will never trust anyone. I feel so low, so completely alone.

As I stare at the ocean, I start to fantasize again about dying. It seems like it would be a relief—a clean break from the flashbacks. And then in the next moment, I worry about how my death would hurt my family. So I push the idea away, not for the last time, and instead I dream about running away, getting away from this house for good.

Survivors of child sexual abuse suffer terribly, and for complex reasons. Everyone agrees that child abuse is horrific, but it is important for both Christian leaders and survivors to understand exactly why it is so damaging, and why the consequences of childhood trauma persist into adult life.

A Bit of Biology

Trauma is the past hijacking the present. There is now significant evidence that maltreatment and chronic stress in childhood affects the development of a child's brain. Our brains continue to grow right into young adulthood, shaped by genetic disposition, environmental stimulation, and experience. The brain has a degree of plasticity, and responds to repeated stimulation, especially in the higher cortex—the part that controls our thoughts and feelings.

The organizing principle for the brain is memory. Our brains have about 100 billion nerve cells that are consistently sending signals to one another. When we are stimulated by an experience, the nerve cells connect, and a neural pathway is created. Depending on the strength or repetition of the experience, that pathway may only be instantaneous or may expand and strengthen until it is encoded as ongoing memory. Of course, there are many minor experiences that forge only a superficial connection between neurons, and which we forget quickly. But major or repeated experiences stimulate the brain to manufacture a larger neurotransmitter, which means the brain is actually growing and changing its shape, consolidating the memory for longer. Most of the time this is a wonderful process, as we learn to walk and speak, operate toys, play sports, and develop skills that soon become "second nature." It's the way our brains learn to comprehend and respond to the world.

But experiences of stress also affect the structure and chemical activity of the brain, and can negatively affect a child's physical, cognitive, emotional, and social growth. They can create deficits in a child's executive functioning, impairing the memory itself and filtering thoughts, impulses, and cognitive flexibility. We now know that children who regularly experience threatening situations become hyperalert to danger and experience overly persistent fear. Traumatic experiences can affect the connectivity between the two parts of the brain, resulting in anxiety or depression in later adolescence, or even altering the ability to generate serotonin, the neurotransmitter that provides feelings of emotional stability.

This biology plays out in our behavior and lived experience. Research now indicates that survivors of abuse are statistically more likely to experience depression, anxiety-related disorders, or panic attacks, to develop eating disorders or substance dependence, to show antisocial or aggressive behavior, and to consider or attempt suicide. There's also a link between many mental health conditions and childhood trauma, and a growing body of research indicating a higher risk of personality, psychotic, and schizophrenic disorders. Many survivors have difficulty concentrating, are constantly on edge, and have difficulty cultivating intimate relationships. Some throw themselves into multiple, almost arbitrary, sexual experiences, while others avoid sex altogether.

In 1998, Dr. Vincent Felitti and his team at the Centre for Disease Control and Prevention published a paper outlining the results of their Adverse Childhood Experience Study (ACE), which surveyed over 17,000 patients. This study has been highly influential and is cited in a report by the World Health Organization on preventing child maltreatment. The study looked at not only sexual abuse but also physical and psychological abuse. It found that child abuse significantly affects survivors into adulthood in tangible ways. Their study found a correlation between levels of trauma and chronic depression, suicide attempts, alcoholism, drug use, domestic violence, obesity, unintended pregnancy, and sexually transmitted disease. Survivors are more likely to have financial problems or skip out on work. The higher prevalence of these things ultimately led to a 15 percent greater chance of survivors contracting any of the top ten leading causes of death in the United States, including cancer and heart, lung, or liver disease.

Childhood trauma permeates adult behavior with long-term consequences: when children are maltreated, they seek out unhealthy coping mechanisms. Coping with trauma is exhausting, overwhelming, and destructive.

A Bit of History

It's quite startling to realize how recently serious attention has been given to psychological trauma, and specifically to sexual abuse, compared to other areas of the medical field. Only in the last century has it been given prominent attention, largely with the maturation of modern psychiatry study. For many years there was a general assumption that little children often fantasize about their parents and make up sexual stories.

For many centuries, symptoms in the area of child sexual abuse were grouped under a broad condition called "hysteria." This was thought to be a mostly a female condition, but it wasn't well understood. In the 1890s several significant psychologists began investigating the condition more deeply, including the famous Sigmund Freud. Freud eventually concluded that sufferers from hysteria weren't crazy or deluded, but were "people of the clearest intellect, strongest will, greatest character, and highest critical power."

Freud discovered that most of his patients suffered from "reminiscences," meaning that they were distressed due to the conscious or subconscious memories of traumatic incidents. His findings led to a treatment process that formed the basis of modern therapy, whereby people can alleviate their distress if they are able to carefully recall the traumatic incident in words.

In 1896, Freud discovered another common pattern: almost all his patients recalled some kind of childhood sexual experience. He wrote an article titled "The Aetiology of Hysteria," which included the statement, "I therefore put forward the thesis that at the bottom of every case of hysteria there are one or more occurrences of premature sexual experience." This was a hugely controversial claim. It became known as the Seduction Theory, which, in short, asserted that the development of our minds during childhood is shaped and nurtured by our experiences. The introduction of premature sexual activity during this process creates effects and thoughts that are incompatible with the central mass of our thoughts and feelings, and therefore can't be integrated, resulting in a traumatized sense of self.

Freud was basically right, and his groundbreaking insight is still heralded by experts today. But Europe was not ready for the implications of Freud's findings. Hysteria was so common in European society that if Freud's theory was true, it meant that child abuse was prevalent throughout Europe, in both upper and lower classes. Of course it probably was, and indeed Freud himself said, "Our children are far more often exposed to sexual assaults than the few precautions taken by parents in this connection would lead us to expect." But other psychologists rejected Freud's findings, and he was isolated. Eventually he retracted his theory and famously turned his focus to other aspects of sexuality and psychiatry, for which he is now more famously known. For various political and societal reasons, other psychiatrists also retreated from this area of study, and that was the end of the exploration of trauma for a long time.

Incredibly, it would take almost another century of wars—with their millions of shell-shocked soldiers—for the area of trauma to be seriously explored. The experience of soldiers prompted more study of trauma in general, until, partly through the advocacy of the feminist movement in the 1960s and 1970s, modern society's attention was slowly drawn to the topic of domestic and sexual violence against women. This eventually led to more political attention directed toward the victims of sexual crimes and the affects of trauma. In 1962, Dr. Henry Kempe published a paper titled "The Battered Child Syndrome," which sparked public outcry at the apparent prevalence of child physical abuse. This led to more specific analysis of sexual abuse. In the 1970s the issue's profile rose through the reporting of abuse in the press, which led to the increase of clinical research on the topic in the 1980s. Advocacy, government inquiries, and reporting in the press have all contributed to the continued rise of awareness of sexual abuse, which in turn has led to increased reporting to police.

Major studies have since confirmed that child sexual abuse *is* prevalent. And the effect of childhood abuse on its survivors was shown to be essentially the same as the effect of trauma on survivors of war. Today, both the prevalence of abuse and the psychologically traumatic effects of child sexual abuse on its survivors is accepted by all experts in the field. The historical inattention to the issue explains the lack of response to the suffering of children throughout history—but this is cold comfort for generations upon generations of traumatized people.

The Experienced Trauma of Abuse

Childhood is a quest to answer the big question "Do I matter?" from a position of total vulnerability. It's the most important question we can ask, and the answer will shape the core of our identity, even into adulthood. We take every interaction and experience to heart in answering that question, and it shapes our growing understanding of our tender little world.

One psychologist puts it like this: "Human beings are meaning-making creatures. As they develop, they organize their world according to a personal theory of reality, some of which may be conscious, but much of which is an unconscious integration of accumulated experience." As we grow, our personality develops and takes shape. It's easy to underestimate how much of a child's understanding of the world is formed in the early years, as nurture builds on nature. Children internalize everything, and every experience becomes a building block for self-identity. They are deeply impressionable.

While sexual assault can happen to both children and adults, the unique dynamic of child sexual abuse informs the resulting trauma both biologically and experientially. In the case of an adult rape, the event usually occurs suddenly and is experienced as a violent shock. Child abuse, however, often occurs over time, and with coercive intensity. The perpetrator is often known and trusted by the child or their family—or is actually a family member. In the majority of cases, the perpetrator has groomed the child before the abuse.

Grooming is the practice of building a trusting relationship with a child through friendly attention, specifically to lower the child's inhibitions for unlawful sexual activity. Sometimes a perpatrator will groom a child for many months. This increasingly occurs over the internet, especially through social media, as well as through normal community networks. Children are lured into actions that are then repeated, sometimes for years. There is often no one shocking moment; instead, there is a progressive dynamic over a period of time, resulting in many instances. This means that the victim is less likely to suddenly react or call for help. Grooming is itself criminal behavior.

Trust is a fundamental principle of healthy childhood development. We grow when we feel safe, and children need to be able to assume the world is a trustworthy place. This means that small children must rely on the adults in their lives to be trustworthy. That trust is a profound bond that ensures the child grows with a necessary sense of security. Thus good parenting and teaching should always include predictable patterns, boundaries, and rituals. The most important ingredient that children need is consistent, reliable love from adults—most importantly, of course, from their parents. This safe love builds internal security in a child and encourages confidence, self-acceptance, and a growing understanding of interpersonal boundaries.

The introduction of inappropriate sexual activity to a child constitutes a massive betrayal of that precious process. The breach of their still-tender personal boundaries is all the more damaging because the child's psychological world is still being formed. Unlike adult trauma—which, though distressing, we can identify as an anomaly in the normal process of life and a clear breach of our well-formed boundaries—child sexual abuse thrusts an entirely new trajectory to the development process. It forces an inappropriate experience upon the child, profoundly interrupting and changing their fragile inner world. Unable to comprehend the reality of what is happening, children find the new and monumental task of adapting to this strange state of affairs incredibly traumatic. It instinctively shifts them into a hypertense posture, an almost permanent state of stress-induced "flight or fight." They respond by trying to muster together what Judith Herman describes as an "immature system of psychological defenses." They do anything they can to cope, and this coping process wreaks havoc on their normal development.

Herman further explains the immediate psychological effects of abuse on a child:

> [Childhood abuse] fosters the development of abnormal states of consciousness in which the ordinary relations of body and mind, reality and imagination, knowledge and memory, no longer hold. These altered states of consciousness permit the elaboration of a prodigious array of symptoms, both somatic and psychological. These symptoms simultaneously conceal and reveal their origins; they speak in disguised language of secrets too terrible for words.

Because the abuse incident is highly traumatic, childrens' attempts to adapt to their new reality cause their minds to behave in ways that profoundly alter their personality. Abused children live in an inner state of hyperalertness, constantly scanning for signs of danger and threat. This is exhausting for a child. It is the very opposite of an ideal context of safety, which nurtures healthy growth.

Abused children experience a profound feeling of helplessness, perceiving their perpetrator as an all-powerful figure. They become deeply fearful of the perpetrator. Additionally, of course, some abuse involves severe physical pain. With no option to escape, many children actually learn traits of extreme compliance and good behavior in a bid to placate the perpetrator. But not every child responds to abuse in the same way.

A fragmented identity. It's common for adults who experience trauma to blame themselves. For example, after a bad car accident we might preempt blame by castigating ourselves, saying things like, "I'm so stupid—I shouldn't have been driving that fast in the rain." This is an understandable way to bring order to the chaos, to frame and clarify the reason for the shock we are feeling. It makes sense: I did something wrong.

For an abused child, however, this self-blame is multiplied to a manifold degree. Lacking the objective worldview to comprehend that the powerful adult is at fault, the child will internally assume that they must be "bad"—it must be their fault. The secrecy the perpetrator creates around the event perpetuates this, especially if they threaten the child with severe consequences if anyone ever finds out. What is happening feels deeply wrong, but abused children assume the blame for it. Even though they are completely innocent victims of a predatory crime, they internally associate all the feelings of "doing something wrong" and "no one finding out" with "I'm being naughty."

It's hard to emphasize strongly enough the traumatic effect that assuming responsibility for such horrific events has on a child. Their growing self-hatred can be profoundly complicated and is reinforced further by any feeling that they initially welcomed the "playing," or if they have had to passively watch their siblings being abused. The assumption of badness, accompanied by feelings of shame and guilt, becomes the default means by which they understand themselves, and this only increases with age. Children can develop the deep internal conviction that they are filthy and worthless to the core. Priscilla remembers, as a child, feeling like a large, black snake was wrapped around her lungs and in her stomach.

One significant reason why children embrace their sense of guilt and worthlessness is to maintain a normal relationship with the wider world, including their parents and other adults. Internalizing the evil helps them feel like it is contained; it allows them to keep living their life. In a world full of powerful adults, it's too overwhelming for a child to consider they may all be bad. But if they themselves are the bad one, then they can continue to cope with the world. The consequences of the opposite being true are unthinkable. This means that some children actually strive to overcompensate for their inner badness and become high performers in a particular area of life, driven intensely to be good. Most, however, are also filled with deep fear. This lack of inner security makes them tend to overcompensate in seeking comfort in the external world, and their inner worthlessness means that the judgment of others plays an exaggerated role in their identity.

So survivors live in two worlds. The outer self, which faces the world but feels less than real, receives all their energy and focus as they try to be good. Meanwhile the inner self, their real self, is a hidden chasm of badness and is marked by fear, anger, and shame. These two fragmented, disconnected selves remain a paradox of tension as they enter adulthood, as the vast majority of their attention is devoted to maintaining the outer self.

Emotional volatility. Children suffering from trauma are unable to fully recognize or even feel the extent of their pain. Their inner world becomes a complex, volatile place. They often swing between reliving flashes of the horrific events and feeling strangely numb. They lose the ability to regulate appropriate emotions and can become dominated by emotional extremes, constantly swinging between heightened anxiety, despair, loneliness, fury, and numbness. They are also likely to experience significant anxieties and extreme phobias. They can fret over what seem to be small matters and develop fears of what seem to be innocuous situations. They are often unable to cope with even minor stresses or pressures. Their anxious rage often comes out in disruptive behavior, including excessive anger or aggression, and they can have a tendency to explode in frustration and violence. The inevitable punishment they receive for this behavior only reinforces how bad they are.

This emotional complexity can also express itself in sleep disturbances, nightmares, or insomnia. Sometimes, as they get older, they will begin to self-harm, learning that an intense physical pain can briefly relieve the inner psychological pain. Survivor children often also develop unexplainable physical medical symptoms. I can recall several nights when my parents called a doctor to address my intense stomach aches, only to find nothing wrong, even as I writhed in pain on the bed.

Abused children experience extreme trauma but lack the capacity to understand it. The pillars of healthy, integrated development—absolute trust, consistent love, clear boundaries, and the growing ability to understand and express feelings—may have been significantly undermined.

Dissociation. These traumatic symptoms have a tendency to become disconnected from their source and to take on a life of their own. This experience of dissociation is when a person mentally detaches from reality for a moment, often in response to stress or trauma. It can be mild, such as daydreaming, or extreme, such as an altered state of consciousness. Children dissociate when they don't feel that the world is trustworthy. They begin responding differently to situations, detaching themselves from present reality for short periods of time. It's like switching off from the present for a moment—a significantly distracted, trance-like experience. In environments of repeated abuse, this can even occur during the abuse act. Usually, however, the child develops a pattern whereby they dissociate on occasions of stress, extreme situations, or moments they would rather avoid. It is essentially a coping mechanism of extreme compartmentalizing. Their emotional capacity is limited as a result of the trauma, so if an experience is too difficult to integrate into their current self, their minds take a step away, as if they were listening to a party from a separate room. This is a learned coping mechanism, indicating the presence of trauma that, unaddressed, will wield incredible influence into adulthood.

Dissociating is something I have done instinctively since childhood, and for years I just assumed everybody did it. I can switch off from the present reality and disappear. We see the character Marcus do it in the film *About a Boy*. Marcus's mother suffers from depression and has recently attempted suicide. At school one day, Marcus so disassociates from his class that he actually begins to sing quietly in his seat, much to his subsequent embarrassment.

Understanding these consequences is vital if we are to offer safe and effective Christian leadership to the people and communities under our care.

The Storm, the Chasm, and the Pain—
Common Experiences of Survivors

Part of the difficulty of explaining the traumatic feelings of abuse is our inability to place them in context. When we have a physical injury, we are helped by the clarity of reason, even when the pain is immense. Those around us can better understand why we are hurting and can offer sympathy.

But trauma is different. Even now, as an adult, the terrifying, swirling mess of my inner world is sometimes hard to comprehend, especially because it is unseen, located in the consequences of past experiences. The physical sensation of carrying the wound feels like a chasm, which fills and overflows too quickly with storms of rage or emotional noise. People speak about having a lump in their throat. I sometimes felt like I had a mountain weighing on my chest or a massive gulf—a dark, empty chasm. I also intermittently experienced something like a blanket of sadness over my mind. Looking back, I can recognize the aching sadness—a very vulnerable feeling, especially as a child. I cried regularly when I was alone, which made me feel strange and silly. At other times I just felt numb. The flashing memories of the abuse stung, and sometimes even took my breath away. And yet the sheer gulping sadness of it all remained somehow intangible. I felt the absence of something, a gaping hole, as if I were antimatter—as if my body marked the spot where there was nothing but emptiness.

I found my experience echoed in the words of Judith Herman, who notes that many survivors describe "a dreadful feeling that psychiatrists call 'dysphoria' and patients find almost impossible to describe. It is a state of confusion, agitation, emptiness, and utter aloneness." Dysphoria is the opposite of euphoria, but it's so much more than just feeling down rather than up. It comes from the Greek words *dys*, which means "difficult or hard," and *pherein*, which means "to bear." The trauma of child sexual abuse is hard to bear indeed. It is a monstrous burden, out of all proportion to anything a child or adolescent should have to bear. The felt experience of trauma can range from panic to despair and everything in between.

But we feel the way we do for entirely valid and logical reasons. Child sexual abuse is traumatizing, and part of our experience of the trauma is not only in regard to our inability to cognitively understand what is happening but also in regard to the strange feelings that accompany the abuse. In his book *The Body Keeps the Score: Brain, Mind, and Body in the Healing of Trauma*, Dr. Bessel van der Kolk outlines how traumatic stress is felt not just psychologically, but physically, "affecting our innermost sensations and relationship to physical reality—the core of who we are. We have learned that trauma is not just an event that took place sometime in the past; it is also the imprint left by that experience on mind, brain, and body." I can still recoil if I am touched on a certain part of my knee. It brings on panic. My body keeps the score.

In these ways and others, our entire lives reflect the impact of childhood trauma. The clinical consensus is that adult survivors of child sexual abuse live with consequences that profoundly affect many aspects of their lives, not only in terms of the painful feelings that dominate our attention but also in the many ways the trauma has become ingrained in our development since childhood and has therefore shaped our behavior, our identity, and our subsequent personality. It can sometimes be hard to distinguish the effects of trauma from other influences of life. Let's look at a few common experiences of survivors.

Flashbacks. Instantly, with no warning, a scene from the abuse act can flash to the front of our mind, and with it come many of the associated painful feelings. It's like being thrown into a parallel moment in time. Flashbacks can happen anywhere: at work, while driving, while watching a film, or—perhaps most disturbingly—during sex. Flashbacks can also be triggered by small details associated with the abuse. These triggers can include anything from a mention of sexual abuse on the news, hearing a certain name or word mentioned, or seeing a certain color or object. These seemingly small details spark an immense emotional response. For many years I would remember images of my childhood bedroom in Traralgon—and then suddenly I would see Greg leaning over me, and the ache of fear or vulnerability would hit like an unexpected punch in the stomach. It was as if the man who repeatedly entered my bedroom was now a semi-permanent resident in my mind. Often these feelings were overwhelming and brought tears to my eyes or sped my pulse. This is a strange experience when standing on the football field, sitting on a bus, or walking through a shopping center. Survivors live with the knowledge that the past refuses to leave them alone.

Nightmares. Many survivors have terrifying nightmares throughout their childhood and adult years. Sometimes they relive the abuse acts, and often, particularly in the years before they realize their abuse, survivors have terrifying dreams with no apparent explanation. The dreams can be about anything;

they don't necessarily include the abuse, but they give an image to the underlying trauma. Often they involve being placed in a horrifically scary situation. As a small child, I recall a repeated nightmare in which I was trying to cross the road right outside our house while a car drove straight at me. No matter how fast I ran, I couldn't get to the other side. At the moment of impact, I suddenly awoke. Years later, after I had realized my abuse but was still secretly determined not to tell anyone, I started having repeated nightmares involving impossible jobs. In one common scene, I was compelled to move a large pile of bricks from one location to another in an unrealistic timeframe. As soon as I began, it all came undone. It was impossible to fix in time, and I awoke, sometimes screaming. It is terrifying to face a trauma in which even sleep is no longer a safe haven from the ongoing marathon of pain and fear.

Panic and anxiety. Many survivors experience ongoing anxiety, particularly when placed under pressure, as when they have to make choices quickly. Others feel it when they are unsure what someone thinks of them. These feelings can express themselves in either avoiding or fixating on food, or avoiding men in particular. Survivors can also experience panicked fear when forced to divert from their regular life routine or when they are separated from their home or a particular partner or parent.

Once, quite recently, I experienced this while boarding an international flight. I generally quite enjoy flying, but on this occasion I was seated in a middle seat, squeezed between two adult men. Right away I felt threatened, and my heart started racing. I stood up and walked back out onto the landing for as long as I was allowed. Despite having looked forward to the trip, everything inside me yearned to be at home in my living room. I could not believe my own feelings. Finally a kind flight attendant gave me some water and some comforting words. With my wife on the phone, I let myself be talked into boarding, and the flight attendant kindly moved me to an aisle seat. Ten minutes later we were in the air, and I was calm, though slightly embarrassed. I have no explanation, except that on this particular occasion, the anxiety of being trapped in that seat between two grown men for a fifteen-hour flight was a real trigger point for me. At the time, it was inexplicably terrifying.

Rage. Many survivors experience instantaneous rage, even from early childhood. Others have an almost permanent, seething resentment. I recall several moments in my childhood when, confronted by what I perceived to be a miscarriage of justice—even in a minor situation, such as a sporting match—I flew off the handle in a rage. I can sense it still. Priscilla can remember twice when she has seen it at its height (thankfully in nonviolent ways). Both times I felt I had been misjudged as having bad intentions in a specific situation. In that moment, something snaps, and adrenaline shoots through my body. In a strange way I feel incredibly alive, pumping with anger, and yet I know I'm probably not quite present. It's the feeling that comes when the circumstances in the physical world collide with the storm of traumatic noise inside. Rage is different from righteous anger, although they are related. Getting in touch with our anger is a topic we'll explore in detail in chapter five.

Fear. Extraordinary, permeating fear is common for survivors, even from a very young age. This is a defining consequence of the fundamental pillar of childhood trust being compromised. Survivors grow up with an instinctive notion that the world is a scary, untrustworthy place, in which unspeakably painful things can and do happen, and they live in anticipation of them happening. The absence of trust promotes a sense of the unpredictability of life, which cultivates a perpetual feeling of vulnerability and hyperdefensiveness. This deeply affects their ability to have sustainable relationships and to face the vicissitudes of life.

Two selves. It's generally understood that there's always some distinction between our public image and the real self inside, but abuse survivors experience this as a much stronger separation. Their identity is often fragmented to the point that their external and internal worlds are almost alien to one another. They have come to see their inner true self as unworthy and bad, and in order to survive they spend an inordinate amount of energy constructing, refining, and maintaining a version of themselves that is more acceptable. Indeed, they can become very attuned to the judgments of others and skillful at adjusting to them, like chameleons. They can spend years behaving in ways that fulfill the expectations of people they've idealized and from whom they seek particular affirmation.

This is an incredibly exhausting way to live—a fact I know from my own experience. I learned to speak and behave in a manner that prompted praise from certain people, and this was how I came to find my primary value. That version of Tim was so driven to work hard—believing that achievement through hard work equated to love—that he because exhausting to keep up with. From the inside, that Tim often felt like a different person, almost a stranger. When I was tired and pulled back, he looked like a shell. But even then, the real Tim inside felt worthless, small, vulnerable, and insignificant. Yet it was this inner Tim who carried the real burdens, felt the big fears, and, every now and then, exploded with rage.

Hypervigilant parenting. Some survivors of abuse only begin to recognize the extent of what has happened to them after they become parents themselves. And, understandably, many become hypervigilant in protecting their own children. They don't let their children stay over at a friend's house, they choose to live in houses where there are no isolated bedrooms, or they insist that their children sleep with the light on. For some survivors, becoming aware of their fear for their children is actually the factor that triggers their moment of realization. Suddenly it clicks: "That's why I do that!" The betrayal of their own trust in childhood instills in them an unconscious overcompensation in protecting their own children. Priscilla and I recognize these hypervigilant tendencies in each other all the time. We constantly find ourselves mitigating against all manner of potential threats to our children—and not just regarding unsafe people. We check, recheck, and triple check locks at night, and regularly retest fire alarms. Our level of trust with others is low and we have had to help each other not to overprotect our children, and not pass on to them a worldview based on fear.

Sexuality. Child sexual abuse can deeply affect our ability to comprehend healthy physical sexuality. Having had their natural sexual development violated, survivors find sexuality incredibly difficult, if not impossible, to navigate. The very feeling of pleasure is associated with danger and betrayal, and the deeply vulnerable act of making love becomes a place of unthinkable vulnerability, almost like revisiting the abuse context. For some, the triggering activity is overwhelming, and it's easier to avoid sex altogether. For others, sex can become associated with the only context where they feel really wanted, and becomes an almost compulsive activity.

Ongoing consequences. When the recollection of our abuse occurs during adolescence—a time already packed with confusing biological and psychological changes, it can make an already difficult time of life almost impossible to bear. The vulnerability of becoming sexually aware even in a normal way fills adolescents with questions and embarrassment, but the confusing, painful memories of sexual abuse introduce shame into this process. Research indicates that adolescent survivors tend to experience depression, low self-esteem, and thoughts of suicide. Among incest survivors in particular, studies indicate higher rates of attempted suicide. Female survivors have significantly higher occurrences of suicidal or self-destructive thoughts, depression, self-harm, and characteristics of hostility. Male survivors are more likely to display behavioral problems, but all adolescent abuse survivors are more likely to be alienated or withdrawn from social environments and interpersonal relationships.

It is not unusual for young survivors to do things that seem irrational to other people. I look back on the year after I recalled my abuse experience as profoundly confusing. Now, with the perspective of therapy and years of recovery, I feel incredible sympathy for that young boy, trying to cope with many of these experiences alone and battling to remain acceptable to the outside world. It made a difficult period of life almost impossible, and the impact continues into adulthood, with both immediate and ongoing consequences.

This Is Trauma

The trauma caused by child sexual abuse is not the same regular adult stress caused by deadlines for work or study (although childhood stress does affect our capacity to cope with normal stress in adulthood). Survivors of abuse have been exposed to an ongoing traumatic event at their most vulnerable age. Herman says that "traumatic events overwhelm the ordinary symptoms of care that give people a sense of control, connection and meaning." A traumatized individual may experience intense emotion, but without any clear memory of the event. Conversely, they may remember everything in detail but without any emotion. This is why they often experience the effects of their abuse even before they realize what has happened. The resulting effect is sometimes diagnosed as Posttraumatic Stress Disorder (PTSD). Posttraumatic stress is a complex condition that affects people in different ways, but the effects are summarized by Herman as *hyperarousal*, *intrusion*, and *constriction*.

Hyperarousal describes the permanent expectation of danger that survivors feel. Sufferers from PTSD constantly anticipate something going wrong. The feeling most people get in a scary movie, or walking in a dark alley, they feel constantly. It means their nervous system is constantly alert; they are always on edge, and the constant adrenaline can have a detrimental long-term effect on their bodies.

Intrusion is the periodic experience of the event intruding on our life. This includes flashbacks and nightmares, but also our apparently inexplicable fear of certain people, rooms, and even smells. We can't always explain it, but there are triggers for our trauma everywhere. I think of it a bit like negative nostalgia.

Constriction is the survivors' impulse to shut out the world, to numb themselves against life. It's like surrender: an exhausted impulse to stop fighting and just block everything out for while. Constriction can manifest itself through decisions to disengage with life's activities, but it also includes the abuse of alcohol, drugs, or other numbing comforts.

You Can't Do It Alone

If you are a survivor, this will be a lot to take in. You may need a few attempts to read it, but I encourage both survivors and Christian leaders to engage the above section. Coming to see that there is a real reason for our complex pain is an important experience. This may be the first time you have ever deeply considered why you feel the way you do. Or perhaps you've have worried about it secretly for years, convinced you were a freak. You would probably be willing to trade anything for genuine, inner peace.

But you're not crazy. You're hurting—and for valid reasons. You have had a highly traumatic experience at your most vulnerable stage of life. You have already endured a long, long journey, carrying a burden by yourself that is unwieldy and unfair. The effects of the trauma since childhood are themselves an indication of your long fight to survive. You are already a survivor, but you are going to need some help.

THREE

BREAKING THE POWER OF SECRETS

When in doubt, tell the truth.

MARK TWAIN

For God has not given us a spirit of fear, but of power and of love and of a sound mind.

2 TIMOTHY 1:7 (NKJV)

TIM'S STORY

By my early twenties I was enrolled in theological college and was fascinated and stimulated by everything I was learning. Emotionally, however, I was lost. Then my girlfriend and I broke up, and everything began to fall apart. My emotions swirled beyond my control. Vastly contrasting moods would overwhelm me, and I started to overthink and doubt my thoughts and feelings. Several times a day I would start crying at random. At other times I could hardly breathe. I stumbled around my college campus, feeling paranoid and lost, yet looking stern and absent. I found it hard to concentrate on anything except my own mental state. I felt out of control. I instinctively knew I needed help.

One lecturer, David, had made a good impression on me in class, not only for his helpful explanation of theology but also for his pastoral sensitivity. He felt trustworthy and safe. I decided to knock on his office door. Later, sitting across from him over coffee, I poured out how I felt, which seemed vastly out of proportion to reality and a little out of control. I wondered if I was going mad. He listened carefully and patiently, not eager to jump in with quick solutions or suggestions. After I had spoken for a while, he made some observations and shared some thoughts, reflecting on his own experience of grief. I felt peaceful with him, and loved by the way he took my crazy feelings seriously. We agreed to meet up again.

In our third conversation I told him I had been abused. He slowly nodded, and continued to calmly listen, his eyes full of attentive care. When I had finished talking he told me how sorry he was, but he didn't overwhelm me with platitudes. I noticed that he was thinking, and he asked me what I wanted to do about it. I replied that I didn't know, so he started to explain what he understood about the options that I had. But he also said he didn't know everything about this area, and asked me if he could seek some advice, anonymously, from an old colleague who was an expert in the field. I felt both vulnerable and relieved, and readily agreed, as long as it was anonymous.

A few days later we met up again. David shared the information and advice from his former colleague, which was helpful and clarifying. We talked at length through various options, and he expressed support for me going to the police when I was ready. Talking with David, I felt calm and in control.

Most survivors don't disclose their abuse during childhood. There are various reasons for this, such as the fear of not being believed and the inner narrative of self-blame and shame. Survivors understandably both expect and dread negative repercussions if they tell someone. And of course they may have been directly or indirectly threatened by their abusers, who often go to extraordinary lengths to keep the secret.

As mentioned earlier, most abuse occurs after a period of grooming, in which the perpetrator builds a trusted relationship with the child through special attention. This coercion is intended not only to facilitate the abuse but also to control the situation and its consequences. Do not underestimate how seductively manipulating a predator can be. Their goal will have been to create a position of trusted power over the child, while maintaining a likeable and respectable reputation in the broader community. In other words, they are grooming and manipulating both the child and the child's adult family and friends. These tactics are invisible to everyone, including the child.

This dynamic is heightened when the abuse occurs within the family unit. For example, if the perpetrator is the father, uncle, or grandfather of the child, a close bubble of trust exists already, shielding the abuse from the outside world. The power of the secrecy is more intense, not only because the abuser has unlimited access to the child but also because his trusted power over the child is already established. In the context of a family unit, the cost of breaking the spell of secrecy is greater, and it results in a deeper betrayal of trust.

The popular film *Meet the Parents* made comedic use of the term "family circle of trust" to describe the particular bond that exists within a family unit. This idea resonates with us because we know that all families have a bond of unique memories, sayings, assumptions, and rituals. We know what happened that Christmas or on that road trip, or where Dad usually sits at the table. We know the way things are in our family. At its best, "the way things are" is a deep knowledge that comes from our belonging to a specific, loving community. But at its worst, it can become a wall of secrecy, a code of silence that keeps dark family secrets contained. Things happen in every family that the outside community never knows. We say things to our family members that we would never want outsiders to hear. These things are usually shielded from the world because of the unspoken family bond. We prefer to keep them, quite literally, "in house." Family secrets can last for decades, even generations. Generally, family secrets are rightly private, but when the health of the family members is compromised through physical, psychological, or sexual abuse, this secrecy becomes a powerful liability. Many survivors reflect later on their "big family secret."

The perpetrator of abuse can maintain a powerful hold over the whole family, who become either direct or indirect victims. Family members might tell themselves, "Everyone loves my dad. He's respected at work and even at church. No one will believe me." The abused family members feel like they are betraying their family by speaking out. It can take a long time before survivors see the truth that it was the perpetrator who betrayed the family, not themselves.

Whether they are inside or outside the family unit, perpetrators cultivate a special bond of secrecy between themselves and the child. This spell of secrecy, maintained through coercion, is incredibly powerful. Survivors live under this spell, isolated and profoundly distressed, for years, even after they come to realize that they were abused. Breaking the power of the spell is tough indeed.

When a Child Discloses

The earlier a child discloses the abuse, the better, since it means the immediate danger of further abuse can be addressed, and because early intervention can begin to mitigate some of the ongoing effects of traumatic stress. But it's rare that children are able to do so.

Some children do disclose the abuse directly or, more likely, they behave in a way that gives rise to suspicion. For example, they might draw a sexualized picture in Sunday school. If there is reason for suspicion, it's important that leaders show calm, attentive concern in a caring manner. They should let the child say what they have to say in their own way, and not ask leading or too-direct questions. The key three words to remember in all such disclosures, with either adults or children, are *listen*, *believe*, and *acknowledge*.

Listen carefully, believe that the person is telling the truth, and acknowledge this to them. You do not have to make a big scene, which may overwhelm the child. This is a very courageous act for a child, and they may think they are doing something wrong by speaking out. Above all, in that moment, they need to know that you have heard them, that you believe them, and that they have done the right thing by telling you. Remember, they are going to have to tell this story again to authorities or child protection workers at some stage.

Be careful, however, not to make overstatements about how "everything is going to be all right" or other promises you cannot guarantee will be kept. This is a complex matter. While everything should be done to ensure that the welfare of the child is the first concern, the matter is not just going to go away. There is a difficult path ahead that the child can't comprehend yet.

While our initial response will naturally be curiosity and righteous anger, research indicates that children provide the most accurate information when they're allowed to narrate freely, rather than being asked direct questions. We must not interrogate the child, looking for them to confirm our suspicions. Instead, as we talk with them, we should allow them to say everything they wish to say. This means we can ask some open, vague questions, prompted by their comments, but we cannot ask leading questions. Avoid yes and no questions. Instead, ask general, nonthreatening questions that assure the child that it is all right to elaborate, such as, "Tell me more about that." Keep it simple and don't drag things out or repeat questions over and over.

As soon as the conversation is over, immediately write down everything you can recall the child saying, in their words. After that, write down the specific circumstances of where and how their disclosure unfolded, with a description of how they seemed. For example, the child might have been "very distressed and kicking toys," or "crying a little while she drew," or "sitting alone near the window all morning."

Next, if you're in a church context, I recommend that you immediately speak with the senior leadership of the church. In any case you should contact the local child protection authority right away. In many places people working with children have a legal obligation to notify the authorities if they have reason to suspect that a child or young person under a certain age has been or is being abused or neglected. Even if that is not the law in your particular state, it is my strong recommendation. To do otherwise is to assume a level of judgment and expertise that is inappropriate and potentially dangerous. Becoming conversant with the law in your local area is essential, as is ensuring that your church has a clear protocol and procedures in place for these circumstances (in line with your denominational body), and that all paid staff and volunteers in your church ministries understand this. Our responsibility to create an informed, safe church community means we must adopt the best practices we can.

When an Adult Discloses

There are few moments in ministry that matter more than how we respond to someone who discloses to us that they have been sexually abused—and the older a survivor gets, the more likely they are to disclose.

Survivors can experience a significant amount of further trauma if they are not believed when they first disclose. As Christian leaders, we must be mentally prepared for this moment, because rarely, if ever, will we expect it when it comes. The person who discloses is often someone we would never have suspected of having been abused. Be mentally and emotionally prepared for surprises, and try not to look too shocked or distraught when it occurs. We can be, and must be, prepared to handle it when it comes. The key words to remember are the same words I mentioned with children: *listen, believe,* and *acknowledge*. Remember, this may be the single bravest moment of the person's life so far. They have already run an emotional marathon to reach this point. They will disclose only when they feel genuinely safe or are desperate.

Be aware, however, that one of the insidious aspects of abuse is that perpetrators have often reassured them that they are safe even during the act of abuse. So for many survivors, being told that they are safe is actually a trigger and can cause enormous anxiety and fear. Your initial posture should be one of calm, reassuring attention. Don't overwhelm the person by sitting too close or hugging them. Sit at or below their eye level and listen calmly and carefully. Your aim in this conversation is to validate their story by carefully hearing it and by showing, by your undivided attention, that you take it seriously. This affords the person respect.

As they tell their story, sit quietly and offer minimal encouragers —nodding, looking them reassuringly in the eye. After they have spoken, don't make them any significant promises about how you are going to fix everything for them, and don't position yourself as a great rescuer. Rather, reply with, "I am glad you told me," and then, "Nobody deserves to have that happen to them."

At this point the person may be timid and hesitant to say more, or they may pour out the whole story. Let them take the lead. If they want to talk, listen carefully. Having stated the essentials, they'll likely feel a mixture of relief and fear at what this means. Remember, your job is not to be their counselor. You are not a therapist. Your role will be to believe them and then resource them. This has been the biggest secret of their life, one that they may have even kept from themselves. Telling you may be the first time they have said the words out loud. They will feel exposed and vulnerable, and they may instinctively regret having told you. You can show them that they have made the right decision by being calm, trustworthy, and reassuring.

With an adult, you will not have a legal responsibility to report to authorities. In fact, it is important that survivors know they are in control of their own decisions. This is a significant part of them taking back control of their lives. One of most difficult things about finally telling someone your big secret is the fear of unknown consequences, and especially of surprises. People who have experienced trauma feel change as a threat. No traumatized person likes surprises. So before you go any further, and indeed at every step of the journey from here, explain to the person their options. They get to make the decisions—your primary task is to empower them to take control of their life. Abuse expert Judith Herman says that "the first principle of the recovery is the empowerment of the survivor. She is the author and arbiter of her own recovery. Others may offer advice, support, assistance, affection, and care, but not cure."

You can do this by listening to them, assuring them of your support, and spelling out their options. Indeed, in this precious, vulnerable moment, I even explain what I'm about to say before I say it. "What I'm now going to do is list the options you have. It will be your decision what happens next, and my job is to offer you some advice, and then support you in your decision."

By disclosing their secret, the survivor has crossed a major line into a new world. In years to come they will look back and divide their life into "before I told someone" and "after I told someone." Having experienced a profound betrayal of trust, they have decided to trust you. This is a sacred offering, which you must receive and treasure with absolute confidentiality.

In the case of an adolescent or teenager, you will have to apply something of both of these approaches. If the person is still legally considered a child, the principles of mandated reporting apply. You must work within the appropriate legal framework. That means you may not be able to assure them of total confidentiality, and you should not make promises that you may not be able to keep. However, you should listen, speak, and relate with them in a manner appropriate to their age, drawing on the approach I outlined above for adults.

Disclosing Your Experience

If you're reading this as a survivor, you may find the thought of telling someone about your abuse terrifying and unthinkable. This is perfectly normal. I know it both from my own experience and from sitting with others. I will be right up front with you—what you decide to do is entirely up to you. But to help you make this decision, I'd like you to read some thoughts to help you reflect on it.

I certainly didn't tell anyone anything about my experience while I was still a child. My dominant belief at the time was that I was being secretly naughty with Greg, for which I would get in trouble because, well, that's what happens when you're naughty. The idea of telling my parents never occurred to me. Actually, though it sounds strange, my sense of naughtiness was less to do with the abuse acts and more to do with not going to sleep when I was supposed to. I knew that what was happening was probably bad, but in my own experience it was not going to sleep that was the punishable offense. Such is the innocent thinking of a child. So when Greg told my parents the next day that I was a "good boy" who went "straight to sleep," I wasn't about to disagree. This contributed to the feeling that I was somehow complicit in the abuse.

Even after I realized what had happened, I still never considered telling anyone about it. For many years, my default mindset was a paradox: I felt my abuse was somehow unimportant, and yet also too big to contemplate—and also, perhaps, that I was unimportant. I certainly felt the enormous pain of the memories, but as the years went by and as I came to understand more about what abuse was, somehow it still didn't register as something my parents would be concerned about or interested in. Not that they were uncaring or disinterested in me—quite the contrary. But, looking back, the mixture of shame and guilt, along with my inability to fully comprehend what abuse was, meant that the chaos of my teenage mind did not lead me to tell them. It was immediately and instinctively a big secret, and like all big secrets it lived inside me, like a parallel world, a whole other place that felt as real as the physical world, and yet invisible to others. It was part of me, entwined in my deepest feelings. It was terrifying, and yet at the same time I assumed others wouldn't want to know.

All teenagers have secrets. We're all trying our best to be accepted by the world and to avoid any hint of external weirdness. This area is already the location of ambiguity, questions, concern, and a little shame. Teenagers are cautious about putting what they feel into clumsy words, especially anything to do with sex or sexuality.

And so I carried the secret within me. My inner world was dark and unpleasant, but also strangely familiar. It was real and close, and often more present to me than the physical world. As long as I kept it a secret, at least I knew it was contained, and I could go on with life. By contained, I mean it was hidden and under control. My instincts told me there was something terrifying about the possibility of it getting out and becoming a huge, unmanageable thing, visible to everyone.

That would be overwhelming. But I am small, and this secret is big, and so I must contain it.

The Spell of Secrecy

This is the isolation of abuse. The victim manages their secret throughout their teenage years, convinced that things would only be worse if it ever got out. In my case, Greg—thankfully—had long gone. But in many cases the secrecy is reinforced by the lies and threats of the perpetrator, still present, who will say anything to maintain the secret. The perpetrator's words, and the self-talk of the child, cast a spell of secrecy that can last much of their life.

Perpetrators will do anything to remain in control and to ensure that the child stays passive and quiet. Perpetrators often explicitly set up the activity as a secret, using either a "positive" comment, such as, "It's our special secret because we're special friends," or a negative warning. This can also move into blackmail or outright threats, including threats of violence, or even manipulative accusations like, "You make this happen; this is what you wanted," or even "You're so sexy, I just have to."

All of this casts a spell over the child, whereby they feel trapped and powerless to speak or act. These lies, together with our inability to comprehend what has occurred, silence us, sometimes long into adulthood. Remember, the abuser will have been manipulating the people around the child as well, cultivating their image as a trustworthy person. This reinforces to the child that while they themselves feel small and bad, and no one would believe them, because the abuser is powerful, popular, and trusted.

When the abuse is within the family, the spell of silence is even stronger, reinforced by the love the child has for the parent or family member. This is a confusing relationship, as they try to hang on to their necessary belief that the abuser loves them, even as they suffer terribly at their hands. In implicit and explicit ways, abusers will have deliberately manipulated things to keep the victims passive and quiet.

Self-Talk

In addition to the words of the abuser, survivors also have to deal with their own self-talk, much of which, while understandable, is not based on truth. It's helpful to name and dispel some common self-talk patterns.

"It's partly my fault." Many sexual abuse victims struggle with this deep conviction. A child's understanding of the world is based on the necessary assumption that the adults in their lives are trustworthy. When this proves not to be the case, they have to find ways to cope. Often they cope by assuming that they themselves are the bad ones. This begins as a subconscious seed, but can be perpetuated in our mind by accompanying "if only" thoughts. Sometimes female survivors blame themselves for wearing too-revealing clothing. Victims might blame themselves for not locking their door or for not saying no. Many survivors blame themselves for their younger siblings being abused. I recall asking Greg not to leave yet, so that I didn't have to go to sleep.

Each and every one of these responses is part of the normal behavior of childhood. But even if it wasn't—even if, for example, you specifically asked an adult to play with your private parts—it is not your fault. The reason sexual abuse is not just a moral wrong but also a crime is that children are innocent to the complexity of sexuality. They are not yet able to comprehend it. Thus it is the role of adult society to protect children until they reach an age when they are able to determine these matters for themselves. An adult who violates that protection bears one hundred percent of the responsibility for the act, no matter what the circumstances are. *It is not your fault.*

"But sometimes it felt good." This is a very difficult matter to speak about. Because our bodies respond to stimulation, and because sexual feelings are inherently pleasurable, the confusing situation can occur that during abuse the sensation of being touched feels good. Sexual organs are designed for pleasure, and as adults, this is how they are appropriately used. Often, cases of abuse are the first time that these new feelings have been experienced by the child. I know this from personal experience, and for a long time I felt deeply ashamed about it. Certainly it contributed to me not telling anyone earlier than I did.

It was only later that I understood that just because our bodies respond to touch does not mean this touch is welcome or appropriate. Indeed, part of the evil nature of abuse is the fact that this arousal is introduced in an entirely inappropriate context. The confusion this creates in the child is part of the trauma, and contributes to a wounded experience of sexual arousal, which sometimes lasts a lifetime. The experience of sexual touch is associated with abuse. The truth of the matter is clear: your body responded as it was created to respond. The act was entirely wrong, and entirely the responsibility of the abuser.

"But it will destroy his life." This is also something I told myself. I took on the responsibility of trying to contain my abuse inwardly. In fact, in my early twenties I initiated a misguided meeting with Greg. He told me that, yes, he was sorry, but that if the secret got out it would destroy his marriage. In that meeting, I actually assured Greg that I wouldn't tell the police or his wife. I didn't want to ruin his life.

But my promise to Greg was misguided. It was a sign that I was trying to carry the responsibility for what had happened. In one sense I think I was trying to avoid causing what would become a "big deal." After all, who was I to stir up all that trouble?

But the legal consequences of our abuse are not our responsibility. It's not our job to weigh up justice. We can't do that. As we'll see in chapter five, justice has its own weight, and the possibility of grace will come after it. The consequences of the perpetrator's actions are theirs to own.

"I don't want to make trouble for everyone." This is something I told myself for years. Even as an adult, married and having received therapy, it was the reason I still had not told my parents. I loved them and had seen them go through some very difficult times. I imagined it would be cruel to put this burden on them, so I quietly determined never to tell. That also meant I had not taken any legal action, even after having disclosed to others. I knew that if it went to court, my parents would inevitably find out—and that would be too much for them. I needed to protect them.

One day, I had a long conversation with a senior Christian leader, Bob. He had recognized a deep resentment in me. It had been prompted by a minor matter, but it had touched a nerve. Bob observed how fragile I seemed when others made presumptions about me. In his kind, wise way, he had put his finger on something.

When I got home, Priscilla could see something was up. I told her what had happened and what Bob had said. I felt strange and slightly out of control. There was truth in what Bob had said, and it tapped into something I didn't understand. Priscilla was looking at me, listening carefully. When I stopped talking, she slowly said something I did not expect.

"I think it's time you told your parents about your abuse."

"I can't do that," I said quickly. I got up and started walking around the room.

"You can," she softly replied. "It's time."

"It would be cruel. They're too old. I have to protect them."

She quietly interrupted me. "No," she said.

She got up and walked over toward me, her eyes fixed on mine. "No," she said again. "It was their job to protect you."

I burst into tears.

Priscilla put her hands on my shoulders. "You were just a little boy."

Something had opened. It was a revelation, a relief. We sat down on the couch holding hands for a long while. I wept softly. I thought about the huge weight I had carried. The pressure of trying to protect my parents. Assuming it was my job to fix the abuse. I began to see that this was a continuation of the same thinking that had me trying to prematurely forgive Greg by myself (a topic we'll explore further in chapter five) and to avoid bitterness.

I was still thinking it was all up to me, that it was my special job to carry it alone, and that if I didn't, I was a failure. As I sat there with my wise and loving wife, I wept for a vulnerable little boy who had borne such a heavy load of misplaced responsibility.

The Power of Shame

Survivors may fear that sharing their secret will expose them before a judging audience. Shame is the public feeling of inadequacy and failure. Even when it is not something we did, we fear humiliation before the beady eyes of others. We fear being exposed.

Shame consists of a dread, a panicked feeling of potential exposure. It can be a debilitating and paralyzing condition. Psychologist Edward Welch describes it as "the deep sense that you are unacceptable because of something you did, something done to you, or something associated with you. You feel exposed and humiliated." It is the feeling of being "less than" in the eyes of others.

Survivors of child sexual abuse can feel deep shame, especially taking into account the feelings of self-blame that can become part of their narrative. Welch further connects shame with three human emotions:

You feel like an *outcast*. You don't belong.

You feel *naked*. Whilst everyone else is walking around with their clothes on, you feel exposed and vulnerable. You are seen, and what other see is not pretty.

You feel *unclean*. Something is wrong with you. You are dirty. Even worse, you are contaminated.

We tend to respond to shame by hiding—trying to be as small as we feel—or through contempt, always ready to lash out. I remember being at school one day when I was a child, when someone suddenly pointed out to me that my pen had leaked all over my face. The whole class looked at me and laughed. I suddenly yelled out a violent threat to the person next to me. I was ashamed and responded with contempt.

Shame only reinforces our determination to keep our big secret away from everyone. It perpetuates a life of fear.

The path to dissolving shame actually passes through the mysterious moments of grace that are only possible when we speak the truth. Once we speak the truth, truth can be spoken to us. One of the greatest gifts we can receive is the gift of skilled, caring people who begin to help us understand our experience. We become empowered with facts and logic, and come to see the reality of the situation. The giant myths in our mind are gradually reduced to their appropriate size. We begin to learn how to care for our tender inner selves.

Shame is isolating; when we join with another in a bond of understanding, the shame is undermined. This can be particularly difficult for men who, feeling isolated in their pain and shame, are statistically more likely to contemplate suicide. Empirical studies indicate that revealing their story to others often stops them from taking that fatal step. Indeed, sometimes reaching rock bottom finally prompts them to disclose. But it doesn't have to be that late. Research indicates that talking to someone about your experience dramatically lowers stress, improves health, and has a dramatic effect on the likelihood of processing and healing.

Ultimately, our shame is addressed when we come to see that Jesus took it upon himself on the cross. We see God's radical act of acceptance in Christ: he sees us exactly as we are and loves us so completely that he died for us. "There is no fear in love, but perfect love casts out fear" (1 John 4:18). So too the fear of loss, abandonment, and exposure begins to dissolve as we come to see the perfect love that God offers, and our deep belonging in it. Nothing can separate us from the love of God.

Some survivors, particularly men, are afraid of being stigmatized because of the fallacy that people who are abused are more likely to abuse others. But this isn't true. Judith Herman notes, "Contrary to the popular notion of a 'generational cycle of abuse,' the great majority of survivors neither abuse nor neglect their children." A 2012 study by the Australian Institute of Criminology found that only 3 percent of male survivors subsequently committed a sexual offence against a child, and concluded, "This is the largest prospective study to demonstrate with confidence that the majority of victims sexually abused during childhood do not perpetuate the cycle of violence by becoming an offender or by the ongoing victimisation of violence." And psychologist Alan Jenkins says,

> Some suggest the experience of victimisation should be regarded as a risk factor. The risk suggestion is speculative and if true likely to be slight. Sexual victimisation does not in itself lead to a significant risk of perpetration of sexually abusive behaviour. Whilst causal factors are not entirely clear, there are risks associated with much more likely factors, including hyper-masculine beliefs

and conditions of neglect with disturbed attachment. It is more likely that there needs to be a range of other factors present.... The popular notion "victim to offender" is a dangerous idea which alarms many people who are already struggling under a burden of mistaken shame in relation to their own victimisation.

While we must remember that a significant number of abuses are not reported, the overarching point remains that the vast majority of survivors do not offend. Indeed, many survivors become hypervigilant in protecting their own children against potential dangers.

First Steps

As a teenager, Priscilla sat watching a sitcom on television. The show's storyline involved abuse, and sitting there watching, Priscilla suddenly realized what had happened to her. Eventually she told her boyfriend, who was kind and listened to her. He encouraged her to tell her mother. Her mother phoned their church minister, who came straight over. He listened and then called the police. Her father was arrested and later convicted and sentenced to prison. It was an enormously courageous thing for a teenager to do. It was not easy. But now, and every day of her life since, Priscilla knows that she made the right decision.

With all my being I want to encourage you to tell someone you trust about your experience. But you are in control. That's how it's meant to be. If the enormity of telling someone seems beyond you at first, consider what might be some constructive first steps. What is something that you could imagine doing today?

After talking to David, my next step was to walk into a police station in the city, just to ask some questions. I wanted to know what I could do before I decided what I would do. I asked to speak to an officer about perhaps reporting an assault, and I was seated in a room with two kind female officers. I told them my story, and they listened carefully. Then I asked what options I had. They carefully explained it all. They told me I could do nothing if I wanted, or I could report what I had experienced, and cooperate toward prosecution of the perpetrator. They encouraged me to report it but told me it was my decision since I was over eighteen.

I didn't do anything further that day. I thanked them and left. But it was a first step, and I was in control. It was years later before I took the next step: I went to the police again and made an official report.

A first step for you might be to call a telephone helpline and chat anonymously with someone. Think of it as a practice run, gaining courage before disclosing in person. Many survivors begin by telling a close friend first, who can then support them as they approach a counselor, a church leader, the police, or another leader in the community. At some stage soon, consider what the next step might be for you.

Breaking the Spell

You can break the spell of secrecy. Because the spell is built on lies, the way to break it is to speak the truth. This is what it means to break the power of secrets. You don't have to be a prisoner to the power of others. All survivors of abuse—Priscilla and myself included—will affirm that speaking out about our experience was a crucial first step in our recovery. It's incredibly scary—but so is going it alone. As we have seen, this burden is too heavy for us to bear all by ourselves.

You are not alone. Everything in the moral grain of the universe affirms your right to tell the truth about your experience. You are free to speak the unspeakable. You are in control. You have the power to break this spell.

FOUR

WHAT DOES RECOVERY LOOK LIKE?

O solitude of longing,
Where love has been confined.
Come healing of the body,
Come healing of the mind.

LEONARD COHEN, "COME HEALING"

Come to me, all you that are weary and are carrying
heavy burdens, and I will give you rest.

MATTHEW 11:28

TIM'S STORY

I walked slowly out of my psychologist's office and into the parking lot. I felt the usual strange, surreal calm. My eyes were red, and my glasses were still a bit wet from the tears. I paused as I came to my car and gazed at a garden bed nearby, with roses, butterflies, and birds. The sprinkler was on, soaking the thirsty garden bed with a fine mist. I could feel the sun on the side of my arm and face, and the breeze blew softly. I lingered, as if time had slowed down and I was free to stay as long as I wanted.

I felt it almost every time after these sessions. A feeling of being more present to myself—awake, alive, and in touch. A feeling of connection. I reflected on the past hour or so, on how skillfully the psychologist had listened to me. He seemed to have endless patience, and then, with just a few words, he named things I could not put words to but had hoped he would. I felt I could tell him anything. It was incredible, just being able to speak the truth. It was a relief.

There were other times when it was very hard. Once I felt like running out. Every time I had a nervous feeling of anticipation when I arrived. Early on I would think about excuses for cancelling at the last minute. Now, I almost looked forward to it.

And then sometimes it was just plain hard work: hard thinking, and hard feeling. Once I was so filled with adrenaline I could have ripped his bookshelf apart. Another time I'm sure my constant swearing should have offended him—but he didn't flinch. Our time always seemed over a little more quickly than I'd hoped. But then, outside, I felt a satisfied exhaustion, like we feel after a good day's work. An hour's crying is just as tiring. Sometimes, instead of leaving, I wished I could just fall asleep in the comfortable chair.

I unlocked my car, got in, and started the engine. Instead of automatically choosing some music, I turned the stereo off. For some reason I preferred silence after these sessions. It seemed to honor the moment more appropriately. "Definitely progress today," I thought to myself. "But there's so much more to go." I felt in control. I wound down my window, turned out onto the road, and drove home.

Recovery is both a wonderful and dangerous word for Christian leaders. We love to see change, to see people recover, heal, and become whole. And we know that a significant dimension of recovery can be found through a relationship with God. But the danger arises when we don't fully appreciate the long, complex path that true recovery involves.

Grace-Filled Moments

My wife, Priscilla, and I have been on a long journey of recovery together. Our journey has involved special moments of progress through the ministry of others, as well as sermons and prayerful encounters with the ministry of the Spirit. God is the ultimate healer, after all, and such moments can be defining for us. These moments can be breakthroughs as the Holy Spirit encounters and empowers us in a divine way. However, unless they are accompanied by further ministry, such "moments" of ministry can lead to the assumption that these climactic moments are the goal, or that they're all that is required. This can, in turn, encourage a dangerous denial of unprocessed trauma.

To assume or proclaim instant healing from complex trauma is deeply unwise. Trauma is complex. It involves a reordering of our mental map and touches on the most vulnerable aspects of our psychologies. These healing moments are grace-filled steps in a long journey, not the end of the journey itself.

If a person confides an experience of sexual abuse with us and asks for our help, we must be careful not to pray for instantaneous healing. Survivors of trauma naturally long for some climactic moment when everything is purged away and dealt with. But we should not encourage that inclination. Instead, we should pray that they would experience the God of all comfort, the powerful Holy Spirit, who will give them the strength to face the path ahead and guide their recovery. Then, following the prayer, we can invite them to meet with us, perhaps along with a friend of theirs, to talk further about how the church can assist with their healing.

We Are Not Their Primary Therapist

As Christian leaders, we may sometimes be the first person a survivor discloses their abuse to—but it is important to recognize that we are likely not the best person for them to walk with down the long path of counseling. We do not have the expertise. I recommend cultivating a list of counselors you can draw from to refer people to for a wide range of pastoral matters.

Each of these people has a different skill set and approach to offer people in different circumstances.

Caring friends

Untrained/volunteer pastoral care in a church congregation

Employed Christian leader

Ordained minister/pastor

Trained counselor

Employed counselor, with a degree, belonging to an accredited association

Clinical psychologist

Psychiatrist

Each of us may see several of these people for different issues that we face. Each has their appropriate place. If you are the first point of call, you must wisely discern who the survivor should engage with for the longer work of recovery. We should be cautious and seek advice before we have developed the experience necessary to discern the appropriate place of referral.

Some church congregations have their own internal counseling center or a team of caring, experienced volunteers who offer pastoral care or prayer ministry. In my experience they can provide wonderful general ministry. However, they should also be trained to recognize when a pastoral matter has complexities beyond their training and experience. They may still have a crucial supportive role with the person, but they must also have the humility to recognize when other skills are required.

We must avoid giving a person with psychological trauma the implicit or explicit message that their healing will be found in a combination of spiritual warfare, persistent prayer, and a faith-filled outlook. This is theological dualism: it separates the spiritual from the physical. It is unbiblical. But the association of psychological trauma primarily with the spiritual realm makes that naiveté dangerous. We must teach our leaders that just as heart surgeons are trained in the intricacies of a specific part of God's physical creation, so too psychologists and psychiatrists are trained in the magnificent and complex patterns of the human mind.

So should we encourage abuse survivors to seek out further help from a specialist. On my list above, I believe number five—a trained counselor—is the bare minimum for survivors of child sexual abuse. We should presume that the trauma is more complex than it appears. Never play the matter down. Instead, believe, affirm, and support the person, assuming that this may be the most significant incident in their life. When you recommend a counselor to a survivor, be sure to provide them with several choices, and then let them decide.

Vital, Quiet Support

After they've seen a therapist, and it is clear you are no longer their primary counselor, you are free to continue playing a quiet, supportive role. Let the survivor know that their counselor is the primary person with whom they should be processing their trauma, but that you are there to resource them in other ways if need be. They may have theological questions they would like help with, or suggestions of books or prayers, and you are free to take the background role of support. Do everything you can to ensure the survivor's trust in you is never breached, and that they never, ever feel any sense of obligation to you. This is about them and their journey. But we must be careful not to allow our conversations with them to delve into areas best explored with their primary therapist. This can become confusing for the survivor and unhelpful for the therapist.

Lastly, be sure never to mention a survivor's experience in a public space, and avoid mentioning it directly when you see them. If you have a quiet moment, you may ask how they're doing, but make sure it's a closed question so they can easily answer with a yes or no, rather than having to give a small-talk answer to a huge vulnerable issue. It can be enough to just pause with them, look them briefly in the eye, smile, and say, "Hello." That reassures them that while you know about their journey, you are not going to forever remind them of their trauma or keep bringing it up. If things go well, you will increasingly fade into the background. That's the goal.

Can We Ever Recover?

Can we ever really recover from abuse? That's the big question. The short answer is, yes, we can.

The longer answer is difficult to accept—but, once we accept it, it will release us into a new journey of recovery. We cannot become the person we would have been if the abuse had never happened. We can't go back. That option is no longer available: our abuse cannot be undone. But we can heal and grow. We can recover our mind, our body, and our life. We can become whole.

Specifically, this means that we can process our trauma and build inner resources to control our inner world. It means that we can become a strong, redeemed, and whole version of ourselves. We do not need to be defined as victims. We are survivors. We have survived, and the path ahead can lead us from surviving to thriving. We can learn to walk unafraid.

This is not an empty or idealistic promise: Priscilla and I have both walked—and are still walking—this journey. It's been hard, but not as hard as staying where we were would have been. It's long, but the good news is that the payoff comes at each step throughout the journey, not just at the destination. It's a journey *of* recovery, not just a journey *to* recovery. We don't struggle along forever in the dark, in the faint hope of some bright relief far off in the distance. Rather, the journey involves moments of insight, growth, and freedom along the way. Each difficult step brings freedom.

What Is Recovery?

Before I go any further, let's stop and carefully consider the word *recovery* for a moment. The *Oxford English Dictionary* defines recovery as "the action or process of regaining possession or control of something stolen or lost." That's quite accurate for our purposes. Abuse trauma certainly can feel like something has been stolen or lost, including our childhood, inner peace, memories, or innocence. To speak of "regaining control" is helpful too, because it's such an important aspect of abuse recovery.

Survivors often feel a need to try and control other matters of life, even small things, perhaps to compensate for feeling so out of control inside. When I'm feeling stressed I often start tidying up the house. Paradoxically, regaining control of our inner world means we feel less of a need to control our external world, and so we become freer. Recovery is certainly about "regaining possession and control of something stolen."

But the best words in that particular definition are probably *action* and *process*. The path of recovery is long, and it does take time, but we mustn't be fooled into thinking that time is all it takes. Hiding away to pass the time won't fix everything. Time doesn't heal all wounds. As Dan Allender reminds us, our problems cannot be resolved until they are squarely faced. "This truth cannot be over-emphasized. Many abuse victims feel their progress of change is taking too long. The assumption is that if God is involved, then the process will be brief and not too messy."

In his famous book *The Road Less Traveled*, psychologist M. Scott Peck offers a very constructive definition of love. He defines love as "the will to extend one's self for the purpose of nurturing one's own or another's spiritual growth." I think that's brilliant, and it fits perfectly with the theological understanding of love we find in the Bible. Peck says that love is a choice, an act of the will, and not just a temporary romantic feeling. Most importantly, he says that love is about nurturing growth: working to bring about the wholeness and flourishing of another, and of ourselves.

Peck says that we do this by "extending ourselves." Attending to the journey of recovery is work—hard work. But it is also a profound act of love. Peck explains that courage, too, is an act of love, since it dares to choose love in the face of fear.

> When we extend ourselves, our self enters new and unfamiliar territory, so to speak. Our self becomes a new and different self. We do things we are not accustomed to do. We change. The experience of change, of unaccustomed activity, of being on unfamiliar ground, of doing things differently is frightening. Courage is not the absence of fear; it is the making of action in spite of fear.

So love involves both work and courage. This is true both of our love for one another, as we extend ourselves through work and courage to nurture their growth, and of our love for ourselves. Choosing to seek recovery, rather than denying my need for it, is an act of love. Indeed, it is a probably the most profound way in which I can love myself. I used to balk a bit at the idea of loving myself. Now I realize that one of the most important choices I have ever made was deciding to remain on the path of recovery, the long process of work and courage, guided by others. Determining to do this courageous work of love is at the heart of recovery. Knowing that other people love and care for us is of great importance, but it is this act of love toward ourselves that is most profound.

This we can do. But, paradoxically, we can't do it alone.

A Map of the Recovery Journey

Because of the diverse ways trauma affects people, the journey of recovery varies for each person. Still, that does not mean it's entirely arbitrary or unknown. There is a wealth of knowledge drawn from many people's experiences that provides a map of the several stages we can anticipate. For example, in her landmark book *Trauma and Recovery*, Judith Herman observes that there are three main stages to genuine trauma recovery. Herman's framework is widely recognized and now forms the basis of textbooks in the field. Her three stages are as follows:

1. *Safety.* Establishing trusted communication, identifying the symptoms of trauma, and managing immediate stress.

2. *Remembrance and mourning.* Exploring and integrating the traumatic memories, as well as mourning the complex loss it has caused.

3. *Reconnection with ordinary life.* Discovering, integrating, and redeveloping the self, as well as learning ongoing coping skills for life.

Herman explains that a successful recovery will be a gradual shift "from unpredictable danger to reliable safety, from dissociated trauma to acknowledged memory, and from stigmatized isolation to restored social connection."

Imagine that picture: reliable safety, acknowledged memory, and restored social connection. That's our destination. These are the signposts on a difficult journey that adjusts and heals our inner world through careful, tender work. It is a real journey, not a vicious circle. It has a direction, a trajectory, identifiable stages, a destination, and, of course, a beginning.

Ellen Bass and Lauren Davis, in their book *The Courage to Heal: A Guide for Women Survivors of Child Sexual Abuse*, break down the path to recovery into fourteen specific stages. Don't worry—this doesn't mean it's a longer journey, just that they are more detailed about the stages. These are not exact, sequential stepping-stones. They are rather a description of themes, moments, and issues that invariably arise on the journey of recovery from abuse trauma. Some will be major, and other less so. But their overview is worth quoting in full to help us get a sense of the big picture:

1. *The decision to heal.* Once you recognize the effects of sexual abuse in your life, you need to make an active commitment to heal. Deep healing happens only when you choose it and are willing to change.

2. *The emergency stage.* Beginning to deal with memories and long-suppressed feelings can throw your life into turmoil. This is a time when emotional pain is intense, the old coping mechanisms are no longer intact, and it may be difficult to function at your usual level. Remember, this stage won't last forever.

3. *Remembering.* Many survivors suppress some or all memory of what was done to them as children. Those who do not forget the actual incidents may forget how they felt at the time or may not fully realize how much the experience has affected them. Remembering is the process of getting back both memory and feeling, and understanding the impact abuse has had on your life.

4. *Believing it happened.* Survivors often doubt their own perceptions. Accepting that the abuse really happened, and that it really hurt you, is a vital part of the healing process.

5. *Breaking silence.* Most survivors kept the abuse a secret in childhood. Telling a safe person about your history is a powerful healing force that can dispel the shame that often accompanies victimization.

6. *Understanding that it wasn't your fault.* Children usually believe the abuse is their fault. Adult survivors must place the blame where it belongs—directly on the shoulders of the abusers.

7. *The child within.* Many survivors have lost touch with their own innocence and vulnerability. Yet within each of us is a child—or several children of different ages—who were deeply hurt and need healing. Getting in touch with the child you once were can help you develop compassion for yourself.

8. *Grieving.* Most survivors haven't acknowledged or grieved for all of their losses. Grieving is a way to honor your pain, let go, and move more fully into your current life.

9. *Anger.* Anger is a powerful and liberating force that provides the energy needed to move through grief, pain and despair.

10. *Disclosures and truth-telling.* Talking about your abuse and its effects with the abuser or family members can be empowering and transformative, but it is not right for everyone. Before taking this step, it is essential that you prepare carefully and wait until you have a strong foundation of healing and support.

11. *Forgiveness?* Forgiveness of the abuser is not an essential part of the healing process, although it tends to be the one most recommended. The only essential forgiveness is for yourself.

12. *Spirituality.* Having the support of a spiritual connection can be a real asset in the healing process.

13. *Resolution and moving on.* As you move through these stages again and again, you will achieve more and more integration. Your feelings and perspectives will start to stabilize. While you won't erase your history, it will truly become your history, something that occurred in your past. You will make deep and lasting changes in your life. Having gained awareness, compassion, and power through healing, you will have the opportunity to work toward a better world.

These stages resonate with the experience of both Priscilla and me. We have revisited them at many different moments over the years.

Two more things are worth noting. First, Christians in particular may find Bass and Davis's comments on forgiveness difficult to accept. Those comments should be read in light of my following chapter on forgiveness in this book. Second, notice again the positive role spirituality can play. Elsewhere, Bass and Davis note that faith taps into the profound need for love, for which survivors—indeed all of us—thirst. So they write, "With this love comes a feeling of belonging, a sense of safety, a deeper experience of faith in your capacity to heal. And this love is not people-oriented. It's based on a relationship that no one can take away."

I am providing an overview of Bass and Davis's stages of recovery, not delving deeply into each one. However, I will highlight some key principles that are important to clearly understand about the recovery journey.

The Need for Safety

The highest initial priority in recovery is for you to be safe. Very little recovery can happen until you feel secure and in control of yourself and the basics of your life. This includes physical safety in your environment and life situation, but also internal safety, as you experience feelings of stress and anxiety.

Sometimes safety begins with simply making sure you're outside the reach of the abuser. This may include moving to another house for a period of time. You may still regularly see the abuser at social or family events. I encourage you to avoid contact at all costs. This doesn't mean you have to say why—you certainly don't owe the abuser any explanation. They may be coercive about seeing you. They may try to pressure you, threaten you, or manipulate you to keep you within their social sphere. You made need to make a significant change, perhaps at a sacrifice. But mustering the courage to do this may be a significant step for you.

Many survivors don't have a complete recollection of the abuse, and may not have even recognized the links from that experience to the way they're feeling today. This is why you need to see a trained and experienced therapist who is able to put a name to what you have been experiencing. This in itself can be incredibly helpful and empowering. When an experience has a name, it is legitimized and confirmed as real. For survivors of sexual abuse, whose very identity and capacity to recognize boundaries has been violated and undermined, this is important.

You may also require a sanctuary: a place you can go and feel safe. Sanctuaries can be mental or physical locations. I seem to have instinctively found such places over the years—simple, quiet locations including, hopefully, in our home. I enjoy the ambience of an art gallery, with thick, high concrete walls and plenty of space. Somehow I gravitate to those kinds of places. Indeed, I am sitting in such a place now, as I write this: a secluded office with thick walls on a large university campus. It's a peaceful space. In therapy Priscilla developed a practice of imagining herself underwater, away from noise, alone and secure. For her, ever the beach girl, this was freedom.

Safety is about not just external factors but also internal. We need to be safe within ourselves. Some survivors gravitate toward self-harm, substance abuse, or other self-destructive behavior, perhaps over a long period of time, to cope with their trauma. In time, we need to learn to soothe our pain in less destructive ways. Ultimately, safety is about a growing sense of peace—a growing confidence in the pattern of our day, and in ourselves within it.

Integrating the Memories

Once a sense of safety has been established, the journey of recovery can move to the next stage, when the survivor tells their story and, with the guidance of a counselor, begins to explore it. It's hard to predict how you will feel at this point. If you've established a safe relationship with your counselor, your instinct may be to suddenly pour everything out, like an unblocked dam. Alternatively, it may be a slow, careful process.

Telling your story can be incredibly difficult, but it goes right to the heart of how trauma is relieved. The very act of speaking reclaims control, as we put into words what has only been shrouded and swirling images and feelings. You can proceed at your own pace. It will take time, and it will be difficult. It is an act of courage.

But it will also be liberating. Before we tell our story, we are constrained by the fear that we will feel worthless if we are vulnerable. This is why trust is vital in a counseling relationship, even while carefully rebuilding the capacity to trust is one of the primary goals of recovery. This exploration of our story shouldn't focus only on the abuse incidents, but on our whole lives, including before, after, and during the abuse itself. I've been staggered by little details that have come to mind that I initially disregarded as irrelevant but which, once I named them, helped me process my abuse. You may also explore nightmares and flashbacks. As this process unfolds, over many sessions, you'll also reflect on the questions that arise. *Why me? What does this mean? Why did this happen?* These are such precious questions and should be honored with time and space.

Telling your story will also involve being guided in thinking through and interpreting what has happened, and what beliefs, myths, and narratives we have adopted over the years in response to it. This isn't the place for a discussion of therapeutic technique, which would be outside my expertise anyway. The process of carefully telling our story, guided by a skilled counselor, alleviates the stress-related results of trauma.

Still, it is important to remember that counseling is not an explosive, cathartic purging that quickly resolves all our trauma. We instinctively want this kind of experience, and scenes in films of "breakthrough moments" can create the impression that trauma can be resolved if our therapeutic experience is intense enough. But this is simply not true. Breakthrough moments do occur, but it is important to see recovery as a journey.

A New Mourning

Remembering naturally leads to mourning. Mourning acknowledges that the trauma has brought great loss. As Herman puts it, "Only through mourning everything that she has lost can the patient discover her indestructible inner life." It can be easier to focus on other distractions than to acknowledge the deep, sad truth of what has been lost. Herman explains that mourning is about letting go of distracting fantasies, such as getting even, or a quick, heroic attempt at premature forgiveness. Grieving is the true path forward, and it is very difficult. It means acknowledging the full cost of what has been taken away. The loss of innocence, the loss of childhood, perhaps the loss of a proper and safe father or grandfather.

This can be a time of deep despair. It is right that we mourn it. Ultimately, however, while this sadness will last a long time, the acute pain of trauma is not endless. Again, Herman explains:

> After many repetitions, the moment arrives when the telling of the trauma story no longer arouses quite such intense feeling. It has become part of the survivor's experience, but only one part of it. The story becomes a memory like other memories, and it begins to fade as other memories do. Her grief, too, begins to lose its vividness. It occurs to the survivor that perhaps the trauma is not the most important, or even the most interesting, part of her life story.

The journey is slow, but it is also liberating and transformative. You can heal and recover from sexual abuse. You can recover your memories, your body, and your peace. The road is hard, but it is not endless, and each step is far better than standing still.

FIVE

JUSTICE, ANGER, AND THE QUESTION OF FORGIVENESS

*Forgiveness is too important to thwart
through excessive expectations.*

MIROSLAV VOLF

*But let justice roll down like waters,
and righteousness like an ever-flowing stream.*

AMOS 5:24

TIM'S STORY

As a young teenager, I loved going to church. I loved the singing, the friendships, and the deep feeling of connection with God. But I especially loved the passionate preaching. I listened carefully, and took notes. I was eager to learn.

But one Sunday evening one of our pastors said something in a sermon that would change my life.

It was a sermon on the importance of forgiveness, centered on the Old Testament figure David and his attitude of forgiveness toward the jealous King Saul. I'll always remember the words of the main point: "Unforgiveness leads to bitterness." It struck me profoundly. To this day I can remember the words, his face, and where I was sitting.

In the car on the way home I pondered this point and realized that in all my prayers to God for healing about my abuse I had only been focusing on my own pain, and had never considered Greg. I had asked God so many times to take away the pain, but had never considered the topic of forgiveness. I hadn't forgiven Greg. Could it be that part of my ongoing pain was a failure to forgive? Was bitterness part of my pain? As we drove into our driveway, I became worried that I was making myself worse by missing this most important step. I quickly decided what I had to do—I needed to forgive Greg. It was my responsibility. No wonder I wasn't feeling any better.

The next evening I went for a long walk. Alone, I sat among the trees as the sun went down and prayed a very specific, formal prayer of forgiveness. I remember saying it: "I forgive him." It felt immense, and I cried a little. I scraped the sign of a cross in the dirt with my shoe as I felt the gravity of the moment. It was a big moment for a little boy, trying his best to do what he thought was the right thing. Now, I thought, things would be better.

That evening would define my attitude toward my abuse for years to come. I had the best motives in the world, but I was struggling to make sense of something I simply could not handle alone. Looking back, I feel deep pity for that young boy, obeying the sermon, trying to do the right thing.

The words of the sermon are not untrue: unforgiveness can

lead to bitterness. Those who refuse to forgive someone for wrongdoing can indeed harbor resentment over many years and become bitter. But there is much more to forgiveness than that.

This important subject, so central to the Christian gospel, needs to be carefully unpacked if we are going to help deeply wounded people become whole. As a young boy I was nowhere near ready to forgive Greg, and I think that sermon did more harm than good to me at the time. And yet, I do believe that wholeness can ultimately include true forgiveness. Let me explain.

A Burdensome Trajectory

The consequences of that sermon were significant for me, very different from anything the preacher imagined I'm sure. That axiom, "unforgiveness leads to bitterness," became a personal core conviction, and it framed many of the decisions I made in the following years. It set up a trajectory whereby I took personal ownership of the ongoing pain of my abuse, without any engagement with the broader issue of God's justice.

I innocently assumed that the best way to get over my pain was to quickly forgive and, hopefully, forget. But the weight of my burden was immense. Remember that I still had not disclosed my abuse to anyone. I was doing deals in my head, looking for a relief. The axiom "unforgiveness leads to bitterness" convinced me that the task was mine to deal with alone. I took on the responsibility of forgiveness because I assumed that my recovery depended pretty much solely on my capacity to forgive Greg.

Instead, this established a burdensome trajectory that lasted even into my adult years. It reinforced the feeling that the ongoing pain was my own fault, and I assumed that it was my responsibility alone to fix things. It also set a pattern in my life of assuming too much responsibility and taking on unrealistic personal tasks with impossible timeframes. I became a workaholic to the point of exhaustion. I came to see that rather than alleviating trauma, the pressure to forgive cultivated it.

Simplistic Sermons

It certainly wasn't the worst sermon I've heard. As a preacher myself, I shudder to think about some silly things I have said. I don't hold resentment toward that preacher, who would never have imagined, and indeed would be horrified by, the way I applied his sermon to my own situation. But I must mention the significant risk of simplistic sermons, which are often enthusiastic statements that deny complexity. No one can say everything in a single sermon, but I don't remember ever hearing other dimensions of forgiveness and justice being explored in other places.

I do think it is fair to say that when speaking on a topic as potent as forgiveness, there are more complex matters to be explored than the inevitability of bitterness. A Christian leader should anticipate that every congregation has people at the receiving end of significant wrongdoing. Every congregation has divorced, abused, assaulted, broken, confused, and angry people. Some comment about the complexity of forgiveness is warranted.

There is a radical call to forgiveness in the teaching of Christ—but precisely because it is such a radical teaching, it needs to be carefully taught in light of the potential for false or obligated forgiveness to be heard instead. If we are going to stand and speak in the name of God from the pulpit, then we have to take responsibility for the way our words land in the lives of those listening. We cannot shy away from matters as important as forgiveness. If we are going to help hurting people to truly forgive, we will do well to acknowledge that this is a complex issue, and it can't be taught simplistically. There are important reasons for this.

Simplistic Forgiving and Forgetting

In Christian contexts, abuse survivors, particularly women, are sometimes put under subtle pressure to prematurely forgive the person who perpetrated their abuse. Of course, the people offering this counsel don't see the forgiveness as premature. They present it as an important step on the path toward "letting go" in order to "move on." This overture is common, and often given with the best of intentions. But our eagerness to encourage quick forgiveness can actually come from our own desire for the person to just calm down and seem all right.

Abuse expert Jussey Verco argues that this subtle expectation for female survivors to prematurely forgive is exacerbated by society's attitudes regarding women and anger. Our culture is not comfortable with angry women. An angry female is often viewed as crazy, selfish, or out of control. Anger doesn't fit our preferred vision of female behavior. Consider how much more likely a woman is to be described as "hysterical" when she is angry—and remember the historical connotations of that word, explored in chapter two. Contrast this with a male image of anger—determined and righteous, so fitting as to form the plotline for many a Hollywood film. The angry man is often the heroic seeker of justice; the angry woman is hysterical.

We must be aware of such underlying cultural tendencies and take care about our motives for prematurely encouraging these women to calm down, forgive, and move on. Research indicates that this pressure, combined with a simplistic understanding of forgiveness, not only delays the person's ability to fully disclose abusive acts but also inhibits their ability to attribute the responsibility to the perpetrator, and contributes to the self-blame that victims already experience.

Jumping to forgiveness prematurely can also become a fantasy of bypassing pain. Judith Herman writes that the survivor can imagine "that she can transcend her rage and erase the impact of the trauma through a willed, defiant act of love. . . . [But it] often becomes a cruel torture." It can also significantly delay or preempt a person's decision to report the crime of abuse to the police. In short, premature pressure to forgive the perpetrator short-circuits healing and can perpetuate the trauma of the survivor.

True Christian forgiveness is a different thing from a quick, self-manipulated determination to forgive, which merely covers over unprocessed trauma and actually restricts healing. True forgiveness requires theological reflection, as well as reflection on psychological health.

A significant aspect of the trauma of abuse is the feeling of powerlessness. To be confronted with insinuated obligations to immediately forgive is to actually have that powerlessness reaffirmed. For survivors, the journey of forgiveness feels like a mountain, and receiving a message that this mountain is their first necessary hurdle to recovery and freedom is disempowering and totally counterproductive. They'll either refuse to start the journey, or, like me, they'll throw themselves into the work of it with such blind force that it will profoundly shape their psychology, and they'll approach the rest of their life like a cliff face. Ultimately, that will breed resentment, not true forgiveness.

This notion of "letting go" and "moving on" has connotations not only of premature forgiving but also of forgetting. "Forgive and forget" is a cliché for dealing with life's troubles, but in the area of complex trauma, it denies the truth: the reality of what has occurred. It is tantamount to a cover-up or denial. Survivors of abuse have experienced a profound oppression of their personal rights, violation of their bodies through deception and possible force, betrayal of trust, exploitation of power, and the tyrannical imposition of secrecy and personal shame. Having broken the spell of abusive obligation, the last thing they need is the imposition of another obligation under the name of forgiveness. Experts specifically note that an obligated, rather than self-realized, approach to forgiveness can lead to excusing the abusive behavior, and may be motivated by the need to placate or accommodate others' needs or wants, or to submit to an ideology—even a religious one—and minimize the true extent of their trauma. Christian ethicist Karen Lebacqz, writing about forgiveness in the context of rape, says that forgiveness is not sentimentality. "It requires the recognition of injustice and redress of injustice. It is based on truth."

Of course we are also increasingly aware of cases where individuals and institutions, including the church, have used outright coercion to cover up acts done by clergy or other leaders. In those cases, instructions to survivors to forgive and move on with their lives carried more explicit warnings to remain silent, sometimes through bribes and threats. This is both sinful and criminal.

The journey of true forgiveness can only begin when the survivor begins to take back the authority for their lives, including their choices. Remember, the first principle of recovery is the *empowerment of the survivor*. This empowerment means a growing self-realization, embracing the freedom to choose actions and the possibilities they represent. True forgiveness is only possible when the survivor is empowered to move beyond feelings of obligation and prescribed behavior. Premature, obligated forgiveness is not true forgiveness. It is a counterfeit.

Premature Forgiveness Disregards the Offense

Premature, obligated forgiveness does not take the act into sufficient account. For forgiveness to be true it must count the cost, and it must acknowledge the full extent of the crime. Premature forgiveness, by contrast, looks away from the crime, and is therefore closer to denial.

I have found the perspective of theologian Miroslav Volf incredibly helpful in this regard. Volf is now regarded as one of the world's foremost theologians. He is also a survivor of war in former Yugoslavia, where 200,000 people were killed, his village was destroyed, and friends were brutalized. He himself endured an extended interrogation, and his father endured a communist labor camp where, his father says, God "found him." Volf therefore brings personal experiences of trauma to his theological reflection. He suggests that it is immoral to move to forgiveness too quickly.

Should we disregard such offenses? We should not—if the distinction between right and wrong matters to us. It is morally wrong to treat an adulterer and a murderer as if they had not committed adultery and murder—more precisely, it is wrong to treat them that way until the offenses have been named as offenses. That's why such offenses should not be disregarded.

This crystallizes a truth we must understand: to forgive is first to condemn. True forgiveness does not pretend the offense did not happen or does not matter or can be quickly forgotten. Rather, true forgiveness necessitates that we first condemn the act as wrong. We must name it. Condemnation is an indispensible part of forgiveness.

Does this sound harsh? To grasp it fully is to grasp a principle that runs with the grain of the universe and that the Bible teaches comes from the very character of God: the principle of justice.

Longing for Justice

In *Mere Christianity*, C. S. Lewis observes that when we listen to people quarreling, we don't just hear them arguing about what displeased them—we hear them appealing to some objective standard that they expect others know about. We say things like, "I was here first," "You promised," or "It's not fair." We appeal to a sense of justice by which we measure the other person's behavior. Lewis suggests that this indicates a shared sense of right and wrong, some mutual hint of the "rules" of life that we expect the other person to be abiding by as well. He concludes, "First, that human beings, all over the earth, have this curious idea that they ought to behave in a certain way, and cannot really get rid of it. Secondly, that they do not in fact behave that way. They know the law of nature; they break it. These two facts are the foundation of all clear thinking about ourselves and the universe we live in."

This human trait of appealing for justice is profound, and while the specific details may differ across cultures and times, there is no place or time *without* a standard. All cultures and creeds innately long for things to be put right. The desire for justice exists wherever there are people.

We observe this most regularly on the news, when cameras wait outside courthouses to greet people who have heard a verdict of some kind. The people who have borne the wound of the crime tell us their verdict of the verdict. They tell us whether "justice has been served," or if it's a "miscarriage of justice." You can see it in the expressions on their faces and hear it in their tone. They are measuring the events by their instinctive barometer, their inner scales of justice. They feel it in their bones. Our inner longing for wrongs to be righted is acute. We all long for justice.

The God of Justice

The Bible teaches that God is the perfect judge, the very embodiment of justice. The Bible contains over two thousand verses that deal with the issue of God's justice in relation to the poor, and the overwhelming thread of God's perfect justice is found in major passages throughout the Old and New Testaments, including, for example, the vision of the Old Testament prophets Isaiah and Micah, the teachings of Jesus in his Sermon on the Mount, and the future promise of Christ's judgment of all people and nations in the fullness of time. We can hear it in the writing of the prophet Amos, who laments the way God's people exult in festivals and songs, but do not address the issue of poverty. He boldly denounces their indulgence, crying out,

> I hate, I despise your festivals,
>   and I take no delight in your solemn assemblies.
> Even though you offer me your burnt offerings and
>   grain offerings,
>   I will not accept them. . . .
> But let justice roll down like waters,
>   and righteousness like an ever-flowing stream.
>   (Amos 5:21-22, 24)

We're used to hearing that God is love. But God is also just. In this passage, God actually sounds angry—because he is angry! We may have assumed that anger is a sin, but it's not. Over six hundred other passages speak of God's anger, or wrath. God gets very angry, so anger itself cannot be a sin. In fact, anger is the appropriate response in the face of injustice. It makes sense that if God is perfect righteousness, then he is angry at unrighteousness. Jesus himself got angry, perhaps most famously in the synagogue one day, after he dared to heal a man with a withered hand on the Sabbath in front of the Pharisees. Mark records that Jesus "looked around at them with anger; he was grieved at their hardness of heart" (Mark 3:5). Jesus was angry at the Pharisees' unjust, legalistic posture in the face of the man's suffering.

We become angry when our boundaries are broken. It is the same with God. God is not losing his temper; rather, God's anger is the willed, visceral response against everything that violates his good creation. This includes acts of sexual abuse:

God is angry about sexual abuse. God's concern for the welfare of children is sufficiently captured in the words of Jesus: "It would be better for you if a millstone were hung around your neck and you were thrown into the sea than for you to cause one of these little ones to stumble" (Luke 17:2).

Some people find the idea of God's anger difficult to comprehend. It seems to clash with our image of a God of love. But God's wrath is a dimension of God's love. When something we love is spoiled, our love is displayed by our anger at what has happened. Because God loves his creation, he is angry when evil (or unrighteousness or injustice) spoils that creation. I find it hard to conceive of a God who loves me but is not angry about what was done to me. That's a God I would find little comfort in, and would certainly find hard to worship. God gets angry because God is love.

I love my two daughters dearly. If any harm were to come to them, my anger would be unleashed toward the cause of that harm. The stronger the love, the stronger the wrath. Getting in touch with our anger is an important stage in our recovery, and recognizing God's anger on our behalf can be an important aspect of facilitating this.

An important aspect of our hunger for justice is anger. Some feel it seething right away, while others take years to tap into it. This is because survivors often spend years feeling the effects of their trauma without realizing its cause. Experiencing hurt without knowing the cause is itself traumatic, and it means that the anger is often denied or misdirected, either at others around them or at themselves, perpetuating self-hatred and a sense of inner "badness." So it is important for us to understand the true focus of our anger and to be able to properly feel it. Anger is a natural response to injustice. It's a valid emotion, and it must be acknowledged.

It may take just a short time or quite a while before survivors get in touch with their anger. This is not a small matter: acknowledging our anger is an important aspect of recovery. At some stage, survivors reach a point where sheer outrage at the way they have been treated finds voice. If it has been denied or suppressed for years, it can suddenly break through with a fury. It's the experience of the body catching up with the outrage of injustice. Ellen Bass and Laura Davis, in their book *The Courage to Heal*, describe anger as the "backbone of healing." Anger signals the moment when survivors place the responsibility for the abuse where it belongs—away from themselves and on the abuser. The penny drops, and the truth of the matter suddenly hits home. *This was wrong—I was wronged!* It's a moment of clarity that "clears the way for self-acceptance, self-nurturance, and positive action in the world." Once they've reached this point, survivors won't be in danger of premature forgiveness. The time of obligation, of feeling powerless, is concluding. Instead they are moving into a new era of what can be called the journey of self-realization: a greater freedom marked by discovering new meanings, possibilities, and options. It is the moment when the process of justice begins to unfold.

Revenge

After they get in touch with their anger, some abuse survivors may have thoughts of revenge. These can come and go in waves and are deeply mixed with other swirling feelings. Some survivors fantasize about enacting revenge on their abuser. This is understandable but not fruitful. We might imagine revenge as an opportunity for relief, but research indicates that playing out images of revenge in our mind actually perpetuates trauma and makes us more frustrated. Imagining revenge can be followed by feelings of guilt that exacerbate our self-loathing.

We have to do something with any desire for revenge without acting on it, and without obsessing over it. We have to come to terms with the fact that there is no getting even. Revenge will not satisfy our anger or relieve our pain: indeed, those who act on their desire for revenge not only have to bear the consequences of their actions but also have to suffer extended and more complicated dimensions of trauma.

In Ephesians 4:26, the apostle Paul writes: "Be angry but do not sin." This is good advice. God doesn't ask us not to be angry. But revenge is a mistaken response to the anger. Paul also writes in Romans 12:19, "Beloved, never avenge yourselves, but leave room for the wrath of God; for it is written, 'Vengeance is mine, I will repay, says the Lord.'" This matter belongs to God. And this is where our understanding of a just God can bring us comfort: justice is God's business, and we can leave this with him. We don't have to be consumed by revenge. God can handle it.

Miroslav Volf says that a nonviolent world, a world without revenge, actually requires a God of justice. The vengeful thoughts and impulses can be resisted and ultimately let go because we know that God is just. Vengeance belongs to God, so we can let it go.

This is itself a controversial principle to affirm. It feels awkward alongside the image of a loving God that we are used to. But Volf explains:

My thesis that the practice of nonviolence requires a belief in divine vengeance will be unpopular with many Christians, especially theologians in the West. To the person inclined to dismiss it, I suggest imagining that you are delivering a lecture in a war zone.... Among your listeners are people whose cities and villages have been first plundered, then burned and leveled to the ground, whose daughters and sisters have been raped, whose fathers and brothers have had their throats slit. The topic of the lecture: a Christian attitude toward violence. The thesis: we should not retaliate since God is perfect noncoercive love. Soon you will discover that it takes the quiet of a suburban home for the birth of the thesis that nonviolence corresponds to God's refusal to judge. In a scorched land, soaked in the blood of the innocent, it will invariably die.

Survivors of sexual abuse may not have been in a literal war zone, but their minds and bodies have experienced trauma. Think about how we feel when we see someone we love hurt by unwise actions or relationships. Do we respond with benign tolerance, as we might toward strangers? Far from it! Anger is not the opposite of love; indifference is. And God is not indifferent to you, or to the sin done to you. When God deals with sin, he names and judges it for what it is. He knows that sin is costly, for he has borne the cost for it himself. God is not removed from the consequences of evil, for his death on the cross demonstrates the fullness of the cost—which we will explore further in chapter seven.

Anger Becomes Righteous Indignation

Being angry, however, is not a permanent state. It is rather a necessary stage on the longer journey of recovery. It should not be bypassed, but neither should it become our home. As psychologist Judith Herman explains, when our rage has been vented in safety, our anger "gradually changes into a more powerful and satisfying form of anger: righteous indignation." Righteous indignation is powerful because it is locked into a broader sense of justice, one shared by the wider community.

When we move from visceral anger to righteous indignation, it becomes possible for us to see that the abuser's crime was not only committed against us, but against the law, and therefore against all the people of our society. In this way our personal justice is actually a social justice. Child sexual abuse is a crime against the entire community, not just individuals.

I found this realization helpful when I was considering the question of whether to go to the police. I reached a point where I saw that the matter was not solely about me. My deliberations on forgiveness were quite separate from the fact that the community expects and deserves to know when this particular crime has been committed. Justice demands that the truth be told, not only to me, but to the community as well, and especially to those who have a responsibility for the safety of the community. They need to be aware of this person's crimes. No person is an island.

Paul affirms this principle. Following his words about vengeance in Romans 12, he says that every person must be subject to the governing authorities, "for there is no authority except from God, and those authorities that exist have been instituted by God" (Romans 13:1). By allowing the authorities to follow through with their duties, we can see justice done without having to enact it ourselves.

When I reported my abuse to the police, I felt a sense of solidarity. The police stood with me, and so did my lawyer. While the process was difficult and long, I came to see that I was not only the victim of a crime but also a witness to a crime against the law, and therefore against society itself. The care and precision with which lawyers have treated my wife and me has been a marvel. When an advocate takes every specific word you say seriously, it has a powerful pastoral effect. I recall sitting with one lawyer as she took my statement, thinking that I would like to offer other people the same attentive, pastoral care she was offering to me.

The communal nature of Greg's crime was reaffirmed at the final step, when a judge awarded "victims of crime" compensation: a certain amount of money awarded in such cases, which also made allowance for expenses involved in the court case. The judge concluded, however, with some direct words that moved me deeply. After reading through the offences and offering his sympathy for my suffering, he said, "On behalf of the people of Victoria, I am sorry for the crime committed against you."

At that moment I felt the true weight of what was being done. This was not just about me; it was justice served by and for us all. The State of Victoria, where I had lived as a child, was expressing remorse to me. It was owning its responsibility for the welfare of its children and taking it upon itself to both hold Greg accountable and formally apologize for the crime committed against me. I had not expected to be so moved by it, but I was. I felt connected to my community. I felt seen. I was not an island, and I didn't have to deal with my suffering alone.

The Possibility of True Forgiveness

When Greg was sentenced, I was invited to submit a Victim Impact Statement to the judge. It was an opportunity to sum up the impact of the trauma that his actions had inflicted on me. I began: "This experience has deeply impacted my emotional response to almost every area of my life."

I then spoke frankly about the nightmares, the guilt, the shame, the pain, the anxiety, the confusion, and the breakdowns in relationships. I wrote about the way it had affected my relationship with my parents, and now my sex life. About how, since childhood, I had bitten my fingernails until they bled. About my physical reaction whenever anyone placed his or her hand on my knee. About the daily triggers and flashbacks, and my hypervigilant and overprotective parenting of my daughters. About the way I approached work, and the subsequent feelings of burnout. About the ongoing feelings of insecurity and inadequacy, and the periods of counseling I'd required. I spoke truth, and refused to play down the cost of the crime. Then, and only then, was I able to write the following:

> I want to make clear I desire no payback or retribution upon Greg. I reported him to face up personally to the incident, and because of the wider concern and safety of society. It must be on public record, I think that is what the community expects and deserves. After encouraging others to do so, I myself must have the courage to state the truth clearly and see it through. As a Christian I believe fundamentally in both forgiveness and justice.

It may be helpful to separate the various components of true forgiveness. Jenkins, Hall, and Joy suggest that forgiveness involves three components, best understood separately:

1. Relinquishment: That is, letting go of undesired feelings, to ease suffering, resentment, or ill feeling toward the abuser.

2. Pardoning: That is, absolving the abuser for their abusive behavior.

3. Reconciliation: That is, re-establishing some kind of relationship of significance with the abuser. This may not be safe or wise at any time.

My initial attempts to forgive Greg, recounted at the beginning of this chapter, showed my desire for relinquishment. I wanted to relinquish my suffering and thought that this was linked to my feelings of resentment toward Greg. But I wrongly assumed that the way to do this was to quickly pardon him. I jumped ahead and tried to absolve his behavior before I had a chance to fully understand it, let alone get in touch with the righteous anger appropriate to it. This is a common experience for many survivors who live lives of obligation. Their trauma is only exacerbated by their attempts to "forgive in order to forget." Many survivors are dominated by "should." Their shame only increases over time, because they feel their big task in life is to forgive their abuser—something they are as yet incapable of doing. This assumption plays directly into the self-blaming narrative that has kept them captive since childhood.

Survivors need to distinguish between their Christian values and the sense of obligation that may have developed over time. Remember, obligatory forgiveness is not true forgiveness. Anger can be a strong sign that we are moving away from obligation. Anger leaves no room for pretense. You don't have to pretend to not be angry. You don't have to pretend in order to accommodate others, or to show you are a wonderful Christian person. You don't have to pretend at all. God is only interested in the truth: in what you are truly feeling.

The true relinquishing of the suffering and resentment—the start of the true forgiveness—will come only when you have, over time, recognized the full wrongness of what has been done to you, gotten in touch with your righteous anger, and identified who was truly responsible. If we jump to pardoning before then, we are excusing the behavior and too quickly agreeing to restitution in order to placate or accommodate others. Real pardoning will involve a free choice, only if and when we are ready. After all, justice is about attributing appropriate responsibility, and true forgiveness does not deny that responsibility, but pardons in full acknowledgment of it.

As survivors move through the journey of realization, and their sense of self is gradually restored, the focus on their abuser will likely decrease. Indeed, they may eventually reach a place of almost disinterest in the person. This is good, since it means their healing doesn't rely on what happens to the abuser, either through a desperate need for revenge or obligated forgiveness. It is a sign of genuine healing, a reclamation of self where the abuser no longer holds a central place. From this place, empowered, free, strong, and unafraid, the survivor may freely choose to consider the possibility of pardoning. They will not be doing it for themselves. Rather, pardoning can be a free step they take, separate from their own healing: not out of obligation, need, or compulsion, but as a generous, undeserved act of grace.

Reconciliation, the third component of forgiveness, may be appropriate in many cases, such as the restoration of a marriage.

However, it is rarely the wise or safe move in cases of child sexual abuse. While a certain peace or finality may be found in reconciliation, it should only ever be initiated by the survivor, and an ongoing relationship is not recommended. The survivor has enough to cope with already, without having to worry about meeting their abuser. Sometimes abusers will manipulate a situation in order to express sorrow and seek reconciliation. If their sorrow and desire for restitution is honest, they should understand that absence may be their best gift. Often the law will facilitate this.

I know how important this distance can be: after more than a decade of marriage, I have never met my wife's father, and probably never will. I think this is for the best. Trust is not a commandment. It has to be earned. Sometimes the most loving act is the withdrawal of trust.

For the Christian, our forgiveness is only possible through Christ's forgiveness. Only a deep sense of God's grace will enable us to take these steps. In this deeply present place, Christ—who dared to love his enemies, and who alone brings divine forgiveness—is carefully at work. In time, we may join in that work too. Volf describes our forgiveness as an echo of Christ's:

> Eventually the time to forgive may come. She may forgive with one part of her soul while desiring vengeance with another. She may forgive one moment and then take it back the next. She may forgive some lighter offences but not the worst ones. Such ambivalent, tentative, and hesitant attempts are not yet full-fledged forgiveness, but they are a start.

If you feel the obligation to forgive weighing on you, remember that forgiveness is God's business. Just let the process of recovery continue, and let the grace and ministry of Christ continue in your heart. When the time comes, your forgiveness will arise from that, without compulsion or obligation.

SIX

WHERE IS GOD?

All the glory that the Lord has made,
And the complications when I see his face
In the morning in the window.

Sufjan Stevens, "Casimir Pulaski Day"

My God, my God, why have you forsaken me?

Psalm 22:1

TIM'S STORY

I was out of state on holiday, staying with friends in a big farmhouse in the country. One morning I awoke before dawn. Immediately my mind was spinning again with questions and doubts. I crept across the bedroom and went downstairs. After quietly making coffee, I grabbed my cigarettes and a book I'd been meaning to look at and crept outside onto the back porch.

I had grown up in a Christian household and had sat through hundreds of church services and Bible studies. I'd gone forward for many altar calls when I was young, listened to many sermons, and sung thousands of songs in worship. But sometimes all of that felt so far away, so distant compared to my recent thoughts and questions. I often felt the close presence of God, but I had big questions too. I was curious. I wanted answers.

Something about the early morning allows big questions to open out and have their space. On the porch, as the first glint of light started to appear, I looked across the paddocks. Sitting barefoot in my jeans and shirt, sipping the coffee, I felt the caffeine embolden my thinking. I lit a cigarette and opened the small book. It was called *Mere Christianity*, by C. S. Lewis.

I read for hours.

Inevitably, survivors of sexual abuse ask the big questions. Of course, as a Christian leader, you have probably wrestled with them yourself. Where is God in the midst of suffering? This question isn't new. Greek philosophers, along with the earliest church fathers and theologians, wrestled with it. An entire strain of theology, called theodicy, is given to it. *If an all-powerful God of love exists, why is there still pain and suffering in the world?* This is perhaps the most significant question related to what C. S. Lewis called "the problem of pain." Suffering exists. So we want to know: is God all-powerful but not loving? Or is God loving but not all-powerful?

This is a serious, reasonable question for anyone, but especially for those who have experienced significant pain. And there are serious, reasonable answers. I'll explore some of the responses to the question below, but first some reflection is warranted on how we might best approach this question as Christian leaders.

The Right Approach

As Christian leaders, it's important to recognize that there are particular times to lean into the philosopher/theologian aspect of our role, and other times to lean into the counselor/pastor aspect. In other words, while it is important that we do the integral reading and reflection on the theological questions of evil and suffering, we also need to discern whether this is really the appropriate response to the person in front of us. Survivors will sometimes ask intellectually substantial questions, but at other times their questions will be more emotionally substantial: that is, cries of the heart that need to be heard, not intellectual questions that need to be answered at that moment.

I've been in pastoral situations in which, in response to people's questions, I've given long theological explanations, without realizing that they really needed something else. They needed the strange comfort that comes from simply asking the hard questions—to ask them, and be heard. The question "Why, God?" comes quickly to our minds. Speaking it aloud is part of our grief. People need a safe place to ask it and an ear that can handle what they have to say. Sometimes we offer a sermon on theodicy when what's really needed is for someone to demonstrate that God is listening.

Having ready answers to complex questions can sometimes make us poorer pastors. We can be overconfident, nodding too quickly to questions and almost interrupting in our enthusiasm to unleash our incredible knowledge. But our knowledge must be framed within pastoral wisdom, which seeks to listen carefully and discern the questions behind the questions. Pastoral wisdom helps us play the long game, avoiding quick and clever answers. We must be students of not only the intellectual world but also the emotional world. We need to appreciate not only *orthodoxy* (right thinking) but also *orthopathy* (right feeling). We develop this by listening carefully and vulnerably to the stories of broken people, until we too hear the question arise inside: "Why, God?"

In a paradoxical sense, we are ready to lead people not only when we have discovered the answers to their questions but when we have wrestled deeply with those questions ourselves. This doesn't mean we have no answers. But it acknowledges that we do not have them all. The posture of a Christian leader is not one of objective discourse, but of a sojourner. In this we imitate Christ himself, who did not come from heaven only to pronounce the right answers, but to identify with our weakness, even unto death. As we adopt this trajectory in our ministry, we begin to truly "rejoice with those who rejoice, weep with those who weep" (Romans 12:15).

If true comfort is to flow from our ministry in this area, we need to have more to offer than just comfort. This is because all true comfort requires a foundation of truth, a substance, which is the comfort's source. C. S. Lewis makes this point:

> Of course I quite agree that the Christian religion is, in the long run, a thing of unspeakable comfort. But it does not begin in comfort; it begins in the dismay I have been describing, and it is no use at all trying to go on to that comfort without first going through that dismay. In religion, as in war and everything else, comfort is the one thing you cannot get by looking for it. If you look for truth, you may find comfort in the end: if you look for comfort you will not get either comfort or truth—only soft soap and wishful thinking to begin with and, in the end, despair.

If we desire to comfort others, we will need to dig into the matter ourselves, well before the questions come. We will need to ask the questions honestly for ourselves, without jumping to how we might explain the answers to others. So a significant step in engaging this matter is to determine to be personally curious about the hard questions that surround God and suffering.

Advice on Apologetics

This may lead us to apologetics, which is the craft of using reason to explain the Christian faith, especially to unbelievers. It has nothing to do with apologizing. It comes from the Greek word *apologia*, which means "a reasoned defense." The word appears in the New Testament in 1 Peter 3:15-16: "But in your hearts revere Christ as Lord. Always be prepared to give an answer (*apologia*) to everyone who asks you to give the reason for the hope that you have. But do this with gentleness and respect, keeping a clear conscience" (NIV).

We should engage substantially with questions of faith and suffering, and have an answer when we are asked the "reason for the hope that we have." The work of historical Christian figures such as Thomas Aquinas, Blaise Pascal, and C. S. Lewis is still available, and there are many good current examples, such as Tim Keller, Ravi Zacharias, Vince Vitale, William Lane Craig, and Alister McGrath, who will help you to become informed on the various approaches to engaging the issue of suffering.

However, in his book *Mere Apologetics*, Alister McGrath advises against the temptation to have a stock, prepared answer on suffering to roll out when required. This is unwise because, first, it risks being mechanical and disconnected from a person's particular circumstance. Second, it can sound too easy, as if the matter were obvious, prompting the person to feel foolish for asking. Finally, a prepared answer to the question of suffering can lead us to miss the real question. Good apologetics is not about giving people answers to questions we assume they have but rather the questions they actually do have.

Our primary objective is always to empower the survivor. Knowledge can be incredibly empowering, and this is our opportunity to be an informed resource. Listen to them carefully and discern the best response.

Don't Get Defensive

There is a difference between a reasoned defense and being defensive. I must admit that, deep in conversation with an old friend about the existence of God and the meaning of life, I've found my passion actually making me agitated as I argued my case. While this certainly proves counterproductive to the task of explaining Christianity, the fact that I became personally defensive about it suggests that I felt personally threatened. If this was the case, it probably indicates that my confidence was resting as much on my own reason as it was on Christ himself. In other words, my defensive posture betrayed my entire argument. I felt under pressure, as if I had something to lose—or as if the existence of God somehow rested on how well I could argue for it!

Remember, it's not about you and your ability to do anything. It's about empowering the other person. They may become heated and angry as they grapple with it all, but that is something you should anticipate and be ready for. The recovery process may call into question the bedrock beliefs of their life, including their faith. If they ask tough questions, don't be paranoid and defensive, but engage them respectfully and calmly, showing that your confidence is not based on your knowledge and ability, but on Christ himself. In every case your answers will be provisional and incomplete. See yourself as standing beside them, not opposite them, asking their questions for yourself and affirming their search. Be honest about the limits of your knowledge. Your task is to help explain, not explain away. They will remember your manner as much as your arguments. Remember that this may be the first time this person is stopping to ask big questions about God. We all live with a working belief, but it can take a crisis for us to stop and reflect on what we have believed all this time.

Whatever happens, it is unlikely that they will continue on as before. A new chapter has begun. It may present as a disillusioning crisis or as a path to a new, more thoughtful understanding of God. Either way, it will take some time to work out.

Preach on Suffering

Therefore it is important that we preach and teach on the topic of suffering in the regular pattern of our congregational life. The hard questions of suffering are not just for abuse survivors, but for everyone. Indeed, our role as Christian leaders is not only to acknowledge the suffering in the lives of the people around us but also to help people to acknowledge it even when they are not experiencing it. It is not just leaders who are called to "weep with those who weep," but all Christians. I know many preachers who err on the side of safe topics, preferring to stay away from difficult ones. This kind of preaching is of very little assistance to the people of God who seek to live their lives faithfully in the real world. Part of our calling as preachers is to bring the "whole counsel of God," even those things our congregations are unfamiliar with or that make them uncomfortable.

Of course any Christian leader immersed in his or her community knows that suffering is everywhere and that sermons and teaching on this topic are always in season. Often, however, when preachers do engage this topic it is in a series on "hard questions," where it gets a single week's attention alongside other topics such as science and evolution, or war and pacifism. We need more than an occasional sermon or a brief answer to the hard questions when they arise. We need solid, informed teaching. Why not take a whole series and explore a comparison between various faiths and their approaches to suffering? Or the ways Christianity helps us in such times? Or preach through the book of Job or Lamentations or the Psalms? This way you'll build up a greater store of teaching in the congregation's understanding and also send a strong message that the church is a safe place to ask questions; this in particular—perhaps more than any single answer—will be the best apologetic to those who are suffering.

So, where is God in all this? I'm not sure if it's comforting or not to know how common this question is. Throughout history the subject of suffering and God's existence has been discussed by philosophers, theologians, and of course myriad ordinary people who, like you and me, have suffered. This question goes to the heart of all the ultimate questions about life, faith, and meaning. In my own journey for answers I have discovered a

rich library of thoughtful material. I can't provide all the philosophical and theological arguments and views on the matter
here, but I do want to share why asking this question has actually strengthened my faith in God.

We survivors ask this question with both our head and our
heart. We want to make sense of it all intellectually, but it's not
just an intellectual question. We feel the question deeply. It's a
visceral question, which springs from our anguish and experience. I've asked it poring over theology books, and I've asked
it sitting on the rocks at my local beach, looking at the waves.
And so I want to share some thoughts on what suffering tells us
about the existence of God. In the next chapter I'll explore how
the Christian understanding of God actually helps us to cope
with and make sense of our suffering.

Some Introductory Thoughts on Apologetics

These reflections begin with the inner sense of justice we referred
to in the last chapter. When we are wronged, we feel a sense of
unfairness. Why did this happen to me? I've sat with others as
they've asked the same question. They didn't do anything to deserve what has occurred. Bad things certainly do happen to good
people, everyday. It's profoundly unfair. But this feeling of unfairness has, in a strange way, helped me in my questions about
God. It's helped me see that the issue of evil and suffering in the
world does not just create a problem for people who believe in
God. It's a philosophical problem for everyone. Indeed, if there
is no God, it's even harder to find a rationale for declaring things
evil. In *Mere Christianity*, C. S. Lewis writes, "My argument
against God was that the universe seemed so cruel and unjust.

But how had I got the idea of just and unjust? A man does not call a line crooked unless he has some idea of a straight line. What was I comparing this universe with when I called it unjust?"

This deep feeling of unfairness, this inner sense of justice, tells me intuitively that child sexual abuse is evil. It is wrong—and you and I know it. But to say this is to appeal to some kind of universal moral standard. What is that standard? Our longing for justice reveals a deep intuition of objective moral truths. The fact that my abuse feels so wrong is a moral judgment, an indication that I somehow know there are ultimate standards of right and wrong, fair and unfair, good and evil. As Lewis concludes, "Unless we allow ultimate reality to be moral, we cannot morally condemn it." To recognize the unjust acts of this world is to point to the existence of objective justice, an ultimate moral reality. This is, as Lewis puts it, a "clue to the meaning of the universe." The fact that I recognize the existence of evil actually makes the existence of a just God more likely.

So Why Does God Allow Suffering?

Those of us who have survived abuse know the suffering we feel is due to the acts of a specific person, and we are left asking why God permitted it. Why didn't God stop Greg from doing what he did?

One way the Christian tradition has understood this is by considering the nature of free will. The God of love has created humanity with a free will, so that we can love freely. Our capacity to love is contingent on our freedom. Otherwise we would simply be robots, our wills predetermined—hardly the basis of true relationship. But in granting us free will, God introduced the possibility that we would *not* love him, and would reject his authority. Richard Rice explains the consequences that logically follow:

> If we ask why God created a world in which suffering was even possible, the answer is because the highest values of which we know, such as love, loyalty, and compassion, presuppose human freedom. God cannot create a world where personal values are possible without giving its inhabitants the freedom such values presuppose. All this means there was a risk in creating beings morally free. There was the genuine possibility that they would fall, and this is where evil began. God's creatures, then, are responsible for evil and its consequences, while God is blameless. Because in an act of personal freedom, there is no explanation for evil. Indeed evil makes no sense at all.

This makes sense to me. It also means that individuals maintain responsibility for their actions. Christianity understands that evil is a corruption of the goodness of creation, not an independent substance in itself. The biblical narrative tells us that God, being perfectly and eternally good, decided to create human beings as an act of love, and proclaimed them good. He bestowed the dignity and worth of his own image on them. As objects of his love, however, we also have the capacity for willful choice. Love is impossible without freedom. If we are forced or compelled to love, then we do not truly love.

Evil, or sin, came into creation through the actions of Adam and Eve, who decided to act autonomously and to become a law unto themselves. Having been created for real relationship, they had the capacity to defy it, and the result is a fallen creation. Humanity still bears the image of God, but it is tainted, inclined toward evil. Paradoxically, by choosing autonomy, humanity became enslaved in sin. Thus evil and subsequent suffering are the result of our own choice.

The question then arises: if God is all-powerful, why doesn't he intervene? Why doesn't he take hold of our will and force us to act differently, and thus remove suffering? Here the Christian tradition draws on the doctrine of the sovereignty of God. The objection, "If God was both good and all-powerful, he would intervene," assumes that because I cannot think of a reason, there isn't one. But as Tim Keller points out, this is a logical dilemma. "If you have a God infinite and powerful enough for you to be angry at for allowing evil, then you must at the same time have a God infinite enough to have sufficient reasons for allowing that evil."

This isn't determinism, but providence. God remains involved with the world he created, and yet humans remain responsible for their deeds. As theologian David Bentley Hart explains, "God has willed his good in creatures from eternity and will bring it to pass, despite their rebellion, by so ordering all things toward his goodness that even evil (which he does not cause) becomes an occasion of the operations of grace."

God works his ultimate will even as he allows humans to act freely. We remain responsible for our actions. Of course God's ultimate plan is significant indeed. "This project is a matter of setting the existing creation to rights rather than scrapping it and doing something else instead," writes the New Testament scholar N. T. Wright. "He will therefore act from within the world he has created, affirming the world in its created otherness, even as he is putting it to rights."

May I Have Another Life, Please?

Over the years, I've often tried to imagine my life without the abuse. So many times I have wondered what kind of person I would have been if the abuse had never happened? I think about the pain, the loneliness, the nightmares, and the tears, and I ponder how much more confident a young man I might have been. Why couldn't I have been *that* person? Why couldn't I have had *that* life instead? Why didn't God create *my* world without such suffering?

Priscilla can confirm that I sometimes obsess over regret. I am forever pondering the road not taken, thinking back over projects and periods of time and evaluating how they might have been better. I point to times in my life I feel were wasted. This tendency draws me to films like *Sliding Doors*, which explores alternative paths—and of course the *Back to the Future* series popularizes this line of imagination. For years I've mulled over the plotline of a possible novel in which the main character has the opportunity to live his life again and again, making slightly better decisions and perhaps living in a slightly better world.

But I've come to recognize that this inclination is partly a result of my trauma. It's a desire for control, not only of the present but also of the past. I find it very difficult to be out of control—again a very common and understandable trait among abuse survivors. But I've never written that novel about the character who has the opportunity to do it all over again, and I probably never will. Putting aside my literary limitations, it is extraordinarily difficult to figure out how to make the story work properly. The scenario is a logical impossibility.

Vince Vitale, a tutor and scholar of philosophical theology at Oxford University, has written insightfully on this point. He explains that our longing for a life without suffering has un-intended consequences. It's obviously impossible, since we cannot live our lives over again; but it is also not desirable, because in that other world—a world without suffering—*you* would never have been born. And this is a problem, because it is precisely *you* that God loves. Vitale explains:

> We picture ourselves in this world of suffering; then we picture ourselves in a world with far less suffering; and we wonder, Shouldn't God have created us in the world with far less suffering? That's a reasonable thought. However, it's a thought that relies on a philosophical mistake. It relies on the assumption that it would still be you and me who would exist in that supposedly better world. And I think that assumption is false.

The slightest change in the circumstances that made up the lives of our ancestors, all the way down to the precise sperm and egg combination from our parents, would mean that we would never have come to exist. Vitale concludes, "We often wish we could take some piece of suffering out of the world while keeping everything else the same. But it doesn't work that way. Changing anything changes everything, and everyone." As difficult as it is to accept, a world where our experiences never happened to us, where the possibility of suffering doesn't exist, is a logical impossibility.

Realizing this, I can see that constantly looking backwards is not helping me accept who I am today. This obsession, in the end, is actually about accepting myself and who I actually am. To wish for another history is to wish myself out of existence.

And yet the Bible teaches clearly that it is me God knows and loves. Consider Jeremiah 1:5: "Before I formed you in the womb I knew you, and before you were born I consecrated you." The Christian understanding of God's love for me makes it a contradiction to entertain an alternative version of history without me, rendered by a different world without suffering. The Christian faith affirms each person as "a present and enduring object of God's love." God does not entertain an alternative version of history in which I don't exist.

These points help us reflect more deeply on our questions, but they do not completely resolve them. I understand that. This is a difficult place to pause, but it's a point we need to acknowledge, and it's a point at which my thinking repeatedly arrives. It would be an unhelpful place to pause, except for one significant factor that remains at the center of the reasons God is the bedrock of my life as a survivor—God has suffered himself, in the most profound of ways. The incarnation, death, and resurrection of Jesus show us that whatever reasons God may have for not halting suffering, it can't be because he doesn't love us or care. It is to those rich depths of comfort that we now turn.

A BROKEN HALLELUJAH

Love is not a victory march,
It's a cold and it's a broken hallelujah.

LEONARD COHEN, "HALLELUJAH"

My father and mother walked out and left me,
but GOD took me in.

PSALM 27:10 (*THE MESSAGE*)

TIM'S STORY

I was sitting at my desk at home one morning while Priscilla took the girls to school. I was feeling low. There were various stresses in life, on several fronts. But recently I had been facing aspects of my abuse to the point that I wasn't sure I could still cope. I looked out the window into the backyard and tried to picture a way of escaping from everything. Some dark options came to mind. Even thinking about them somehow felt like a relief, an escape. I looked down at my laptop and clicked through photos of my family. There were random shots from the past, crazy fun moments that felt light years away. I knew I couldn't leave my family. I knew that wasn't right. And I knew in my head what was happening to me, but that didn't ease the storm. The idea of escape was compelling. I felt my body sinking, and my mind rolled the curtains of dysphoria down over my eyes.

Hearing Priscilla return, I stood up and walked over to her in the kitchen. I put my arms around her shoulders and, feeling the warm familiar feelings and smelling the familiar scent, I broke down and cried. I wept the desperate tears of despair. After a while, we sat down side by side on the kids' toy box. I continued to cry intermittently as the waves of sadness rolled over me. As we sat there, I searched my mind for distracting thoughts. Ways to change my life from here on. How could things be different? "I want a simple life," I said, but I wasn't even sure what that meant. Work, shopping, speaking, friends, music, writing, cycling, films, food—it all felt trivial and distant.

"There's nothing," I spluttered. "Nothing that really matters at all." We sat there, gazing down at our feet, and the floor. We stared at nothing, and didn't dare to look away. Stuck in a moment we couldn't get out of. No distraction was strong enough.

"Nothing really matters."

And then, in silence, my mind began to reach down, deeper into my inner world. It reached down into the deepest place, where nothing but the most honest and pure aches of the soul survive. The dark, still kernel of my innermost being. And there was the familiar image of my God, nailed to a cross, smeared in blood. I felt the silent, reassuring presence of the Spirit in the darkness. I knew that in the end, that's all that was left. That's it—that's what I need. That's what matters.

In the second year of our marriage, Priscilla began experiencing depression. It usually began in the mornings when she awoke. She found it harder and harder to bring herself to get out of bed. Sometimes at night, too, she would slip into bed early and disengage from all conversation. I tried hard to be a good and comforting husband—which usually meant that I asked her in a hundred different ways what was wrong and how I could fix it. I fretted quietly about her silence and the despairing comments she would make.

One evening my best efforts seemed to be falling particularly short. I offered verbal reassurance and comfort, and generally tried to talk Priscilla out of feeling what she was feeling. Eventually I ran out of comments and, feeling totally anxious about my failure to help at all, lay next to her on the bed and stared at the ceiling, worrying in silence. We lay there for a few hours, feeling helpless. Finally I guess we went to sleep.

The next day, Priscilla suddenly thanked me for loving her like I did. I replied that it was a strange thing to be thanked for, and anyway I was pretty hopeless at it, since I wasn't much use in her pain. She replied, "Last night was wonderful. You were near me, and you didn't try to fix it. That was what I needed."

That sounded ridiculous to me. Being both a husband and a minister, I thought that my life's vocation was basically to fix everything. But I had lots to learn.

In his book *Let Your Life Speak*, Parker Palmer explains that the sympathy of well-meaning friends can be counterproductive. Some try to cheer us up, pointing out what a beautiful day it is. But that only makes us more depressed. Knowing it's a beautiful day but being unable to appreciate it exacerbates our sense of disconnection. Other friends try to remind us what a good person we are—but that is all the more depressing, because we know the gap between who we really are and the persona that others see. This merely reinforces the belief that if they saw who we really are, they'd reject us.

Then Palmer says that there are some who say they said they knew exactly how we feel. But, he declares,

> whatever comfort or counsel these people may have intended to speak, I heard nothing beyond their opening words, because I knew they were peddling a falsehood: no one can fully experience another person's mystery. Paradoxically, it was my friend's empathetic attempt to identify with me that made me feel even more isolated, because it was overidentification. Disconnection may be hell, but it is better than false connections.

Palmer says that this experience, combined with his own feeble attempts to comfort others, showed him that these attempts to fix someone else's suffering were essentially all about avoidance and denial. One of the hardest things to do, he writes, is to be present with another person's pain without trying to fix it. Instead, we ought to "simply stand respectfully at the edge of that person's mystery and misery. Standing there, we feel useless and powerless, which is exactly how a depressed person feels."

This principle is counterintuitive. We feel uncomfortable around others' suffering, and so to resolve and escape our discomfort we offer advice and platitudes. But one of the most courageous and powerful acts of ministry is to let ourselves feel useless near a suffering person. By remaining respectfully near them without trying to fix anything, we impart the life-giving knowledge that someone sees them. "By standing respectfully and faithfully at the borders of another's solitude, we may mediate the love of God to a person who needs something deeper than any human being can give."

As Christian leaders, our inability to fix the trauma of survivors allows us to embrace the role of the sojourner, standing respectfully and faithfully on the edges of suffering. In this way we mediate the ministry of God to others. By holding still in that faithful position, we do the hard work of love— the kind of love that, as Palmer says, "neither avoids nor invades the soul's suffering. It is a love in which we represent God's love to a suffering person, a God who does not 'fix' us but gives us strength by suffering with us." The feeling of being understood, of knowing that someone sees us and is willing to embrace the uncertainty of remaining with us and identifying with us is powerful. This is true ministry, modeled by our God in Jesus Christ. Ultimately, it is only God himself who can move into that space, into the midst of our suffering, and bring healing.

Let Sadness Take Control for a While

My friend Brad and I once took our children to the cinema to see the animated film *Inside Out*. The story shows the inner world of a little girl, Riley, and features her emotions—Joy, Sadness, Fear, Anger, and Disgust—who are personified as characters who live in her mind's headquarters. Riley's memories are depicted as little balls, colored according to whatever emotion they carry and stored in Riley's subconscious mind. The main character, Joy, tries to stay in control of things, even as the other characters step up to threaten and disrupt the balance—all except for Sadness, who seems lost and purposeless. As the story unfolds and things begin to fall apart in Riley's outside world, her inner world begins to fragment, throwing Joy into a panic.

At one point, Riley's emotions meet Riley's imaginary friend, Bing Bong, deep in Riley's subconscious mind. Bing Bong is very upset. As Joy wonders what to do, she is staggered to see Sadness sympathize with him without trying to cheer him up. To Joy's amazement, this actually helps him.

Soon things get very dire indeed, and Riley's "personality islands" start to collapse. Just as a total disaster seems imminent, Joy sees some old, sad memories of Riley's, and realizes that Sadness was crucial to Riley's ability to process and move on from those situations. Back at Riley's mind's headquarters, Joy turns to Sadness and says, "It's up to you."

"Me?" replies Sadness.

Joy pushes Sadness toward the control console, but Sadness is unsure and nervous. "I can't, Joy!" she says.

"Yes, you can," Joy replies. "Riley needs you."

Sadness slowly approaches the control console and tentatively takes charge. This has an immediate effect on Riley, who breaks down and admits her feelings to her parents. Soon, a new memory ball arrives. This one is both blue and yellow—a mixture of sadness and joy—and is stored away in the core memory section.

By this point in the movie, I was a mess. Sitting at the end of the cinema aisle, I hid behind my popcorn. Tears soaked my face and fogged my glasses. Kids' movies aren't supposed to be this powerful. But as Sadness slipped into the control seat, some-thing moved deep within me. I was undone. I looked along the aisle at my daughters and Brad's children with popcorn and drinks everywhere. I saw their innocent little heads gazing at the screen. Breathing heavy breaths and feeling the glorious sweetness that follows a cry, I sat in peace and a mess of popcorn as the rest of the film played out. I could have sat there all day. Sadness had been allowed to take control for a while.

Why don't we feel that way in church more often? Why isn't sadness allowed to take control for a while? Except during occasional national tragedies, joy is well and truly in control of our congregations—though sometimes it is a rather forced joy. We forget that tragedies are unfolding all the time, hidden in people's inner worlds. The Christian faith has rich resources for grief and suffering, and yet our gatherings are too often dominated by a forced joy. The headquarters of Riley's mind at the beginning of *Inside Out* is actually a pretty accurate analogy of the culture of many of our congregations. Joy dominates because everything else is perceived as a threat. I've already addressed the topic of anger—but doubt, sadness, and lament are too often sidelined in the bright, thin norms of our church culture.

I remember an enthusiastic worship leader's invitation one Sunday: "This is the presence of God, so let's leave all our problems at the door, and come in to his holy sanctuary to worship." Secretly struggling with the memories of my abuse, I felt totally unable to do as he said. Leave my problems at the door? Not that I wanted to sing about my abuse, of course, but I certainly didn't feel able to leave my problems at the door. Why not acknowledge the wider, fuller breadth of all of life and affirm the presence of God right there in the midst of it all? As Christian leaders who want to take our ministry to survivors of sexual abuse seriously, we need to make room for a wider spectrum of experiences and emotions, including sadness. This can have implications for our preaching as well as our worship, and subsequently for the culture of our communities.

Should Worship Always Be Happy?

What we call joy is often forced happiness. In some churches this is expressed as distant politeness, and in others, sheer enthusiasm. But in any context, focusing on only one emotional dimension in gathered worship is simply unbiblical.

True joy is not the absence of suffering, sadness, or grief. It is a deep assurance and delight in the fact that God knows and loves me, separate from my efforts and failures. Joy knows very well the extent of suffering, and comes as a balm, not a distraction or denial.

Marianne Meye Thompson, a New Testament scholar at Fuller Seminary, describes true joy as "the effusive expression of gratitude and praise that flows from a resolute, trusting heart that is suffused by hope in God." This description of joy is different from happiness, which is a short-term feeling that rises and falls with our circumstances. In our enthusiasm to portray the good news of Jesus and to be a welcoming church, we can flatten the gospel into merely an enthusiastic spirit of infectious happiness. But that's not good news to anyone—except those already having a bouncy good morning. It's especially not good news to those suffering trauma in isolation and wondering whether God (or anyone else) understands how alienated and anxious they feel. Our churches should be deeply joyful places. They should speak of God and the world in terms that generate genuine trust and hope, which come only through a full awareness and immersion in the complexity of real life, including suffering.

Our churches should be places of truth, giving voice to the deepest experiences of humanity. Even a casual glance through the Bible demonstrates this tradition. Nowhere in Scripture do we encounter platitudes. Rather, we encounter the grit, pain, dysfunction, and sheer joy of life with God. We see Moses arguing with God, Job crying out in anguish, the prophets thundering and weeping over Israel, and Jesus raging through the temple with a whip. We encounter all of creation groaning and a majestic God so full of love that he chose a cradle in a muddy shed as the location for his redemptive revelation. And then we see the cross, to which we will return momentarily.

Nowhere do we find this rich picture of all of life more comprehensively than in the book of Psalms. We should perhaps look a little more closely at the psalms as a model for our worship.

Psalms of Lament

The book of Psalms is the songbook for the people of God. To read the Psalms is to read the lyrics to a music collection, a poetic library, and a soundtrack to life. Though they were written hundreds of years before Christ, the Psalms were sung by the early Christians, and they have been ever since. Jesus quotes them as well—indeed he mentions them more than any other book of Scripture, and they've been correctly referred to as "the songs of Jesus." The Psalms cover the full spectrum of the circumstances of life, including every human emotion. They are particularly powerful for the realistic way they reflect our inner world. Old Testament scholar Bernhard W. Anderson, summarizing Athanasius's comments on the Psalms, wrote that "the Psalms have a unique place in the Bible because most of Scripture speaks to us, while the Psalms speak *for* us . . . by expressing the whole gamut of human response to God's grace and judgment and thereby teaching us how to pray." Indeed they do.

The book of Psalms could actually form an alternative soundtrack to *Inside Out*, since Joy, Fear, Disgust, Anger, and Sadness all get their own psalms. Our tendency is to look only to those psalms that help us praise God or offer familiar assurance. There are, of course, psalms of deep comfort, which we treasure. But we often overlook the several dozen specific psalms of lament—in fact, we may be surprised to learn that there are more lament psalms than any other kind. A lament is a passionate expression of grief, and the lament psalms are packed with grief and anger. Their inclusion in this holy songbook in God's Word should be a great encouragement to us. It is an incredible affirmation of the importance of expressing our pain and grief not only to God personally but also as part of our corporate worship. Tim Keller notes the importance of engaging with the lament psalms:

> The psalmists, despite their intensity and shocking candor, always pour out their white-hot feelings to God. No matter how angry and despondent you may be, if you use the psalms of lament to give you words for your prayers, you will in no sense feel stifled or "bottled up." Rather, the language of the laments is so startling that they will probably help you to be more honest about your emotions than you would have been.

Lament helps us speak truth to God about our deepest feelings. The lament psalms never cover up or deny the true state of things, no matter how horrendous. Indeed, they throw the promises of

God back at him, demanding answers. *Why have you forgotten me? What can I say those who demand to know, "Where is your God?"* And these are the songs God himself has given us.

Todd Billings reflected on this in his book *Rejoicing in Lament*, after he was diagnosed with cancer. As he felt his body break down and endured the pain of chemotherapy, he too felt the sting when songs of sorrow were bypassed in worship. He found what he needed in the Psalms.

> On the one hand, we are to lay open our hearts—with all of their half-formed desires and uncomfortable emotions—before the covenant Lord. Yet on the other hand, the Psalms don't offer us a cheap form of "therapy" that simply expresses emotions for their own sake.... By the Spirit, we bring our anger, fear, and grief before God in order that we may be seen by God.

The honesty of the Psalms helped Billings realize that God saw him as he was. The practice of engaging the Psalms is a response to God's invitation to fully and honestly express our heart's hidden anguish, since God is indeed listening. This, in turn, helps us know that we have been seen by God—a knowledge that is powerfully inclusive and embracing. Being seen by God implies that we have also been accepted by God, that we can rely on God. It offers the profound hope that God is in control.

Consider Jesus on the cross, crying out, "My God, my God, why have you forsaken me?" (Matthew 27:46). Here Jesus is doing what the people of God are to do: he is crying out a psalm of lament in the midst of his pain. In this case, Jesus is quoting Psalm 22:1-2:

> My God, my God, why have you forsaken me?
>> Why are you so far from helping me, from the words
>>> of my groaning?
> O my God, I cry by day, but you do not answer;
>> and by night, but find no rest.

Jesus needed a psalm of lament in his time of suffering. It was not a sign of overt negativity or a lack of joy. It was a truthful cry of relationship. Jesus worshiped through sad songs. He was not stoically holding it all in; he was talking to the only one who listens to everything. Pouring out white-hot feelings to God is the kind of frank honesty and fierce conversation that God invites us into. It is this kind of honest dialogue that is essential for people in anguish. Consider the honest vulnerability of Psalm 6:6:

> I am weary with my moaning;
>> every night I flood my bed with tears;
>> I drench my couch with my weeping.

I've been there. I can relate to that. People with trauma know that the feeling of mourning can be so heavy and last so long that we grow weary from it.

My wife, Priscilla, reflects that in her toughest times, she always turns to the Psalms. We've both enjoyed the music of bands like Sons of Korah, who put the words of the Psalms to beautiful and tender folk music. Hearing these—especially the laments—is moving, powerful, and worshipful. That's why God gave us the lament psalms: because we need them.

Worship in a Minor Key

In 2014, Taylor Swift released her pop album *1989*. It was a global smash hit, dominating the radio and winning the Grammy for

Album of the Year. I'm not really what you'd call a Taylor Swift fan, but I am a fan of the alt-country artist Ryan Adams. Adams is down the other end of the music world from Taylor Swift, but in 2015 he made a surprising move. He recorded a track-by-track cover of Taylor Swift's *1989*. Interestingly, however, he reimagined and re-created the songs as slower, sparser tunes, often set in a minor key. His covers transform the music, summoning doubt, ambiguity, and uncertainty, adding a new dimension to lyrics that had bounced along on Swift's album.

Philosopher James K. A. Smith reflected on Adams's cover album on his blog, pointing out that "when you listen to Adams's cover of Swift's album, you finally realize how incredibly *sad* it is—that buried down beneath the perky melodies and auto-tuned precision of a pristine sound is a lyrical world of heartbreak, disappointment, and despair." Smith then makes the excellent point about how this can be an analogy for our church worship:

> We live, you might say, in a major chord culture. We live in a society that wants even its heartbreaking lyrics delivered in pop medleys that keep us upbeat, tunes we can dance to. We live for the "hook," that turn that makes it all OK, that lets us shake it off and distract ourselves to death. And this cultural penchant for a certain sonic grammar seeps into the church and the church's worship, so that we want songs and hymns and spiritual songs that do the same. But as a result we often create a (*pre*)cognitive dissonance between the Bible's honesty, carried in our hymns and psalms, and our pop retunings. Or we embed them in a sonic liturgical environment that endeavors to be, above all, "upbeat" and positive—a weekly pick-up encouraging you to just "shake it off."

In other words, our worship can distract us, rather than leading us to honesty before God. For those who are experiencing suffering, this is not worship or ministry or healing—it's actually more like denial. Smith continues,

> But then a Ryan Adams comes along and takes you back to lament, and reminds you of all the minor chord moments of the biblical narrative, and invites you into a sonic environment that actually tells the truth about the broken world you live in, and that your neighbors live in, and that refugees from Syria live in. Worship should be a proclamation that tells the truth, not just lyrically, but sonically. And that means music that resonates with broken hearts. Even though the Gospel exhorts us to "lift up our hearts," sometimes that only happens because God in Christ comes down to meet us in our brokenheartedness. That will sometimes happen in song.

As survivors of trauma, we have the ongoing option to choose music that distracts us, or music that moves us. Sometimes I do enjoy music that distracts me, that takes me to another place that is happy and blissful. But I can't remain there all the time, and certainly not in worship, if it's to be truthful to my life experiences. We need worship in a minor key.

The Importance of Mourning

Trauma always includes loss, and as recovery unfolds the full dimensions of loss become more apparent. Sometimes it can be easier to be angry than to be sad. Sadness is so vulnerable and feels so empty. We need ways of helping ourselves grieve. In his book *Raging with Compassion*, pastoral scholar John Swinton explains the importance of lament for helping us grieve over the way life really is. He includes lament in his five practices of redemption in the face of evil, saying, "Lament gives a voice to suffering and releases rage in a context of faith and compassion. In doing so, it opens up the possibility of life and liveliness in the face of forms of evil that would seek to destroy both."

We need songs to sing at such times. The Irish and Scottish cultures know this well and have a traditional practice called "keening," which is a vocal lament or cry for the dead. It is a very old practice, dating as far back as the seventh century, and often occurs during the wake following a death. Bono from U2 referred to it when he spoke about having to sing each night following the death of his father. "I guess I did my grieving for my father keening in front of twenty thousand people singing U2 songs. They really carried me, those songs and my three mates. After the shows I felt much better." He grieved through keening—lamenting.

U2's music can be good for keening, especially the song "40," which takes its lyrics directly from Psalm 40. Its slow, melancholy yet infectious music feels somehow eternal:

I waited patiently for the Lord
He inclined and heard my cry
He brought me up out of the pit
Out of the miry clay

This is followed by the refrain, "How long to sing this song?" which has often closed U2's concerts over the years. Often the crowd continues to sing the refrain long after the band has left the stage. This aspect of their musical repertoire has allowed U2 to facilitate moments of significant public lament—such as in Auckland, New Zealand, in 2011, where they played a concert on the day of mourning following the death of twenty-nine miners in the Pike River Mine Disaster. Their performance drew comparisons with the biblical lament tradition by some colleagues of mine. It included an invocation, a description of distress, overt petition, and finally expressions of confidence and hope. It's the frank, unguarded acknowledgment of the awful truth of sudden death that is so powerful. Laments allow us to speak the unspeakable, and to accept the truth as it really is.

I'm not saying we should have major services of lament regularly for all kinds of suffering. I'm saying that lament can be added to our worship in sensitive ways to provide people who are aching from all kinds of trauma with a place to come regularly before God and do as God has invited us.

Death is awful. Trauma is awful. Sexual abuse is horrendous. And so we must grieve it. Ultimate recovery from trauma must involve acknowledging the loss, which can feel something like a death. The loss of innocence, the damaged childhood. These must be lamented. We won't be able to honestly sing about our glorious hope in Christ until we can sing honestly about the suffering, the pain, and the loss. God knows this and provides for it.

The Ministry of Advocacy

One night sitting on the couch, Priscilla looked up and casually informed me that she had decided to give away all her colored clothes. From now on, she would wear only black. I smiled, but didn't think any more of it until a day or two later, when I went into our room and found her in the midst of bagging up all her clothes. I looked at the hangers left on the rail: just a black skirt, a black dress, and a black cardigan. Below them sat two pairs of black jeans. Everything else was gone.

She started to explain. "The other day at work, I was sitting and talking with an elderly lady living with dementia. Her husband had died, and she was sad and confused. Then she looked at my black dress and suddenly said, 'Oh look, you're the only one dressed for the funeral.' I know it's strange, but as a chaplain, I feel like I want to identify with that person every day. Every day, whenever someone is hurting, I want to be their person in black."

I looked at her and smiled. "You know Johnny Cash has a song about that?"

Priscilla looked confused. "It's called 'Man in Black,'" I said, and grabbed my phone to play her the track.

"Well, you wonder why I always dress in black?" Johnny starts out, and his deep baritone lays it all out in each verse. He wears black for the poor and beaten down, the sick, the hungry, the lonely, and the old. These are the people he stands with.

Ah, I'd love to wear a rainbow every day,
And tell the world that everything's okay,
But I'll try to carry off a little darkness on my back,
Till things are brighter, I'm the Man in Black

Priscilla was amazed, and shed a couple of tears. "That's me. That's exactly what I mean." We listened again, and lingered over the beautiful lines. "I wear the black in mourning for the lives that could have been." Cash is talking about young men killed in war, but there are other ways we mourn lives that could have been: lives that have been stolen through abuse, and lives that are damaged through the subsequent trauma.

Priscilla's quiet advocacy by wearing black is a statement of identification. She sees her ministry as one of identification and advocacy, to make a small symbolic statement of standing with those whose inner world is black. It's a simple yet strong example of the ministry of identification and advocacy, following the model of Jesus, who chose to be identified with those on the margins—the forgotten, the outcasts.

You might wonder whether something symbolic, like wearing black, really makes any difference. It may not change the world, but it can influence the tone of our churches. It sends a message. As Christian leaders we have a significant profile and influence in our community. Our temptation is to associate with those perceived as successful and powerful. We can be quick to share pictures of ourselves with influential people. The pressure to be perceived as a successful or attractive Christian leader can be subtle but real. We can end up simply modeling the culture's happy images, enjoying our blessed, prosperous life. But what if we made some radical decisions about who we choose to be identified with? Our decision to be a safe, informed church that stands with those who suffer speaks loudly about our understanding of the Christian life. And, of course, there are more explicit ways to get involved in advocacy, by learning about how sexual abuse has affected your local community, supporting survivors who are seeking justice, and raising awareness of the issue.

The New Testament scholar N. T. Wright declares that the gospel calls the church to "implement the victory of God in the world through suffering love." We are painfully aware that the church has not always acted in this way. At times, it has become part of the problem of evil rather than a witness to its cross-shaped solution. Trauma survivors feel deep humiliation and suffering. Are we willing to stand with them in humble, suffering love? Can we lead a church that is, in the words of Stanley Hauerwas, a community of care actually able to absorb evil and terror? Such a community is, in the end, the true apologetic for Christianity.

A Traumatic Cross

At the heart of Christianity lies the powerful truth of a God who is all-powerful and yet has suffered. This paradox is revealed at the crucifixion of Jesus Christ. In that event, an eternal God of perfect love and justice acts in an astonishing display of grace, unlike anything in any other religion or worldview.

The God revealed in the Bible is not distant or dispassionate. He can—he has—identified with the worst human suffering through Jesus Christ. This captivates me. The sheer humility and vulnerability of an eternal God dying on a cross for the sin of the world is incredible. This God suffered for me.

God is the ultimate reality of love and justice, and in him every person lives and moves and has their being. He is the very foundation of being and consciousness. How would we expect that God to deal with evil? The idea that God did it by joining with humanity, becoming part of his creation, and taking the position of the despised, the weak, and the vulnerable is astonishing and magnificent.

The Christian faith teaches that we can't truly cope with the suffering of this world or of our own experience until we come to see that God has actually suffered *for us*. Encountering the truth of the suffering of Jesus is transforming. A God who dies for his people is viscerally compelling, and the Spirit of God ministers to our spirit through this truth. It melts and heals our hearts. Jesus suffered and died. God became the embodiment of trauma, for me.

We've become quite used to seeing images of Jesus on the cross—so much so that the brutal force of that wretched event can get lost. But crucifixion was an immensely traumatic way to die. It was the drawn-out, public torture of a helpless victim. It was a cruel and disgusting spectacle. Victims were often beaten or mutilated, sometimes beyond recognition, even before they were nailed to the cross. Soldiers would often crucify victims in unusual positions for their own amusement and treat their bodies in degrading ways. The foot stands on crosses were meant to help victims push themselves up to breathe, sadistically ensuring that they died slowly. Afterward the victims' bodies were often thrown to the dogs or onto the city rubbish dump. It was a brutal punishment, usually reserved by the Romans for those who had defied their authority. In other words, it was an enforcement of tyranny.

That Jesus was crucified naked is not something we often think of, probably because we are so used to seeing him depicted with a discretely placed loincloth. But this was not likely at all, and several early historians mention nakedness in crucifixion. It was a humiliating public event, designed to maximize shame. Sometimes the victim's family would be forced to witness it. The nakedness was intended to humiliate the victim. There's a recurring theme in Scripture of the importance of covering nakedness, since clothing was symbolic of honor, and the Israelites were a chosen, honored people. Biblical scholar Michael Trainor observes, "In keeping with the status of Israel's people it was God's intention that nakedness should be covered. This emerged from the theological conviction that the people of Israel were no longer shamed or disgraced, but a beloved and covenanted people."

The Genesis narrative speaks to this. In the beginning, God created man and woman in his image and blessed them. The writer of Genesis tells us that they were naked but "were not ashamed" (Genesis 2:25). After sin was unleashed into the world, however, they suddenly recognized their nakedness and felt shame for the first time, actually hiding from God. But notice what happened next. Just before God banished them from the garden, there is an unusual verse that tells us, "And the LORD God made garments of skins for the man and for his wife, and clothed them" (Genesis 3:21). I love that little detail—God made clothes for Adam and Eve to cover their shame! It's a little grace moment, foreshadowing a much larger one to come. Thus began the process of grace that finally culminated in Jesus Christ's suffering and death on the cross.

At the cross Jesus took on our shame, represented by his nakedness. For the Jews of the day, crucifixion was unthinkably shameful. Jesus took on that shame for us. His naked, beaten body hung there for all to see. We can be released from our shame when we recognize that God not only sees us as we truly are, but identifies with us. The Lord of the universe has come to stand with us. Our fear of exposure can be dissolved when we recognize that God was exposed in our place.

God is not unfamiliar with trauma. In the garden of Gethsemane, Jesus actually sweated blood as he prayed (Luke 22:44). *Hematidosis* is a rare condition in which blood actually seeps from the skin. It is known to occur to people in conditions of extreme stress, such as just before their execution. Jesus was under extreme trauma, not only because of the physical suffering that lay ahead of him but also because of the sheer weight of what he was about to do for humanity.

Consider also the rejection Jesus experienced. One disciple betrayed him. His closest disciples repeatedly fell asleep when he asked them to pray for him, and when he was arrested, they deserted him out of fear for their own safety. He was left in a public courtyard where he could hear people lying about him. He was spat on, blindfolded, and punched. Peter, one of his closest friends, publicly denied him three times. The feeling of rejection must have been immense.

He was kept awake all night, and early the next morning he was again flogged publicly. The soldiers mocked him by putting a purple robe on him and pressing a crown of thorns into his head. He was so weak by this time that he could not carry his own cross to the execution site, which was the normal practice for crucifixions. My lecturer, David, once impressed this last detail on me as I struggled alone, feeling the weight of my complex trauma: *Jesus didn't carry his own cross alone.*

In Mark 8:34, Jesus says, "If any want to become my followers, let them deny themselves and take up their cross and follow me." Jesus is emphasizing the enormity of the call of discipleship. Discipleship is not to be bargained with or tried out in half measures. Becoming Jesus' disciple will reorder our whole lives.

It can, however, distort into the cliché that "we all have our crosses to bear," as if life is about stoically plodding on alone with our individual burdens. That's not what Jesus meant. The phrase "Take up your cross and follow me" grows significantly in nuance when we fast-forward to the crucifixion and see that Jesus needed help to carry his own cross.

A stoic path of denial through suffering is not the way of Jesus. Greek philosophy and our modern Western culture of manhood alike find honor in "grinning and bearing it," but Jesus models a different way. This little detail, that Jesus didn't carry his cross alone, brings out a theme that resonates through the whole narrative of the crucifixion: that the Son of God experienced shame, nakedness, trauma, and abuse. His physical body, his mental state, and his public image were reduced to filthy rubbish. In the garden, Jesus cried out to God in blood-smeared prayer, and he didn't stop bleeding until the end of the next day, when he died.

In taking the sin of the world on himself, Jesus was dealing with the root of evil. But he was not only dealing with the root of sin; he was also bearing its effects. Tim Keller explains:

> Only through weakness and pain did God save us and show us, in the deepest way possible, the infinite depths of his grace and love for us. For indeed, here was infinite wisdom—in one stroke, the just requirement of the law fulfilled *and* the forgiveness of lawbreakers secured. In one moment, God's love and justice were fully satisfied. This Messiah came to die in order to put an end to death itself. Only through weakness and suffering could sin be atoned— it was the only way to end evil without ending us.

This is God's love revealed most fully: crucified, dying a traumatic death.

Whenever I despair, I look to these images of Jesus. Jesus is my trauma survivor. God went there before I did. I find the sacrament of Communion deeply comforting, and it is the brutality of Christ's death that makes it so. Communion is the meal Jesus gave us, and it reminds us of the fullness of his death. First Peter 2:24 says, "He himself bore our sins in his body on the cross, so that, free from sins, we might live for righteousness; by his wounds you have been healed." When I come to the table of Communion to receive Jesus' body and blood, I experience the work of Jesus in ways I cannot fully explain. I know in that moment that I am not alone in my pain. Communion associates my trauma with a larger event that lies at the very center of the ultimate matters of justice, love, wrath, and the condemnation of evil.

In Communion I am connected to God beyond hymns, sermons, meetings, and buildings. In it I am assured of forgiveness for my own sins. For I am not a sinless person, and I too need salvation. That I come to see myself honestly before God, never condemned, and yet trusting in his justice over all matters beyond my reach, is a mystery of faith that his Spirit alone enables.

The Christian tradition refers to one dimension of the work of the cross as *Christus Victor*, Christ the Victor, which means that in his own death, Jesus paradoxically gained victory over the power of evil and death. This moment of seeming failure, horrible trauma, and death is actually the moment of victory. Death played its full hand on Jesus and was exhausted. In his resurrection, Jesus is vindicated, rising to life, victorious. As followers of Jesus, we share in that victory and in that new life. N. T. Wright summarizes it like this:

> Jesus suffers the full consequences of evil: evil from the political, social, cultural, personal, moral, religious and spiritual angles all rolled into one; evil in the downward spiral hurtling toward the pit of destruction and despair. And he does so precisely as the act of redemption, of taking that downward fall and exhausting it, so that there may be a new creation, new covenant, forgiveness, freedom and hope.

There is more to the Christian theology of the cross than this, but relevant to our reflections here, I find it a compelling way to think about my own experience of abuse. Jesus' death and resurrection inspires me, a survivor of child sexual abuse: it liberates me, restores me, sustains me, fills me, and compels me.

Many of us in the West find our lives defined by innumerable choices, and we feel we have control over what happens to us. If we have the luxury of living by our own choices, we often expect the universe to deliver for us, and we're shocked and disillusioned when it doesn't. But the existence of the majority of people in history, and indeed most of the world, is controlled not by choices but by circumstances.

Survivors of trauma can identify with those people. Survivors do not live with the illusion of control. Instead, a profound part of our lives has been defined by a circumstance we didn't choose. We feel out of control. To have experienced trauma is to know that a good deal of what everyone accepts as normal life is based on circumstances beyond our control.

It's easy to assume that if we are not in control, no one is. When we look at the evil around us and the trauma within us, it's very empowering to know that what happened to us was sin. It wasn't my sin, but it was sin. It wasn't a random, meaningless act that no one can judge. It was an insidious system that allowed a vulnerable person to be preyed upon.

So trauma survivors can find genuine comfort in the fact that the evil of this world stands under the judgment of God. It is of great comfort to know that God judges and condemns sin, and out of love he has sent his son as a sacrifice to deal with it.

A Sure Hope

Communion doesn't just look backwards, remembering the cross; it also looks forward, in anticipation of the renewal of all things. Christian faith is not optimistic, relying on luck—it's hopeful, relying on God. Optimism is merely a positive outlook, which can involve a denial of reality, unhelpful for trauma survivors. The people of God are never merely optimistic, as if the future depended on their ability to maintain a sunny disposition. Rather, we are oriented by hope: a conviction about God's plan for the world, a coming reconciliation, and the renewal of all things.

The Christian understanding is that, because of what Christ achieved on the cross, all of creation is heading toward redemption. The New Testament sketches the promise of a future which is not otherwise possible, but which is now our sure and certain hope. God presents a vision of a redeemed and transformed world, where what Jesus achieved through the victory of the cross is now being implemented.

The path of Christian hope is one not of escape but of the transformation and redemption of this world. The vision presented to us in the book of Revelation, especially chapter 21, is vivid:

> "See, the home of God is among mortals.
> He will dwell with them;
> they will be his peoples,
> and God himself will be with them;
> he will wipe every tear from their eyes.
> Death will be no more;
> mourning and crying and pain will be no more,
> for the first things have passed away."

> And the one who was seated on the throne said, "See, I am making all things new." (Revelation 21:3-5)

The book of Revelation is an apocalyptic vision (*apocalypse* means "uncovering"), and its symbolism points to a new life. It's the life of the whole creation redeemed. It is a just, righteous world, a world put to rights. The God of justice unveils the new world of justice, the God of love a new world of love. To quote N. T. Wright again:

> The New Testament invites us, then, to imagine a new world as a beautiful, healing community; to envisage it as a world vibrant with life and energy, incorruptible, beyond the reach of death and decay; to hold it in our mind's eye as a world reborn, set free from slavery of corruption, free to be what it was made to be.

Christian hope means that God sees us today in our brokenness, but from the perspective of what Christ has achieved on the cross.

Thus he sees not only who I am today, but who I am becoming as he heals and restores me. God sees the deep brokenness of my trauma, but from his perspective it does not define me. I am not, in the final view, just an abuse survivor. I am redeemed. I belong to God. I am a new creation. That is my sure destiny—for the new heavens and new earth are not a vague spiritual place for our souls only. They are a redeemed physical world, with healed bodies and minds. All the recovery that we can experience on earth is only a foretaste of the fullness of all God has created us to be.

EIGHT

CHOOSING LIFE

For freedom Christ has set us free.

GALATIANS 5:1

Help me when I fall to
Walk unafraid

R.E.M., "WALK UNAFRAID"

PRISCILLA'S STORY

When I moved into adulthood, I left home and traveled out of state for a fresh start in Brisbane. I was alone and free in a big city, thinking about how I wanted to make my way in the world. My father had been sent to prison. I still felt the effects of trauma. I had flashbacks every day and was exhausted from the years and years of struggle.

I was in college and got a job working the late-night shift at a McDonald's in the nightclub district. That was an eye-opening experience. I met many people my own age who were obviously enjoying life as much as they could, but who were also taking great risks. Something about that lifestyle appealed to me, and I admired their dangerous, careless freedom. I had complex thoughts about my own inner world. Over time, though, I saw people make poor choices that took them down destructive paths. I decided that was not really freedom.

After a while I gradually concluded that being free wasn't just about doing what I wanted—it was the ability to choose good things for myself. I had been badly wounded, and I felt like I'd been through the worst of life. I didn't want any more suffering. I was sick of it. Even though life was difficult, I realized I could still choose a different life for myself.

I remember the moment well. Early on a Saturday evening, walking down the mall toward work, I decided to choose life instead. I decided I wasn't going to do anything that would damage me or cause devastation to my life. I wanted a path and friends that would help me to become well, to become whole. I decided to choose life.

"It never ends." Those were the first words I ever heard her say. I was sitting in the first lecture of my final subject at college. The lecturer welcomed us and announced that each week she would start the class by inviting a student to share a quote or axiom, based on their experience, for her to write at the top of the board and for the whole class to reflect on for a few minutes. That's when a girl near me put up her hand and suggested, "It never ends."

It seemed too negative. What a thing to say in a counseling skills class, where we'd come to learn how to help people! *It never ends?*

But at the lecturer's invitation, the girl began to explain. While we do believe in recovery and healing, she said, we must also be honest and remember that the consequences and implications of brokenness go on far longer than we may be prepared to admit. She explained that in our life and ministry, we must be careful not to try to wrap things up too easily or impose an artificial order on things. Instead, we should discern true healing as it evolves.

I couldn't argue with her brutal honesty. Indeed, I thought it was quite courageous to make such as stark point in the first five minutes of the first lecture. The lecturer was nodding as she wrote the quote on the board. *Who is this person?* I wondered. But then the girl made a second point. "The other truth is that God's grace and love never end, either. 'It never ends' is a hopeful statement too, about the faithfulness of God. God does not give up on us, and he's always at work in our healing and flourishing, no matter how complex our pain is. The transforming love of God—it just never ends."

The girl was, of course, Priscilla, and "It never ends" has become something of a motto for our life together. Faced with wave after wave of difficult circumstances and challenges, not to mention the underlying trauma from our individual experiences of abuse, we've often had to remind one another, "It never ends."

So what about trauma from abuse? Does it ever end? Yes, it does. It ends all the time. In the journey of recovery, we change and grow and heal, and so our experience of the trauma changes.

But it doesn't end all at once. Complex trauma requires patient healing. It can feel like it never ends, but staying on the journey is the only way forward. It is long, but each step of the journey ends something. There are new challenges in the next moment, and the one after that. Trauma tends to repeat on us. But as we do the good work of recovery, it repeats differently, and so we make progress.

As we do the good work of recovery, with help from those around us, the trauma is ending all the time—and of course the healing grace of God never ends. Even in the midst of Lamentations we find comforting words:

> The steadfast love of the LORD never ceases;
>   his mercies never come to an end;
> they are new every morning;
>   great is your faithfulness. (Lamentations 3:22-23)

I'm still on the journey of recovery, and so is Priscilla. We are learning to walk unafraid. And so I want to share with survivors some things that you may find helpful on this journey. It's a collection of hints and advice from our own experience that will help put the wind at your back as you walk along. For Christian leaders, these are helpful things to know as you support, advocate for, and minister to those walking the journey of recovery.

Ask for Help (Again)

Long-term recovery means giving ourselves permission to ask for help any time we need it. We must recognize that even if we are traveling well, and perhaps have ceased counseling for a season after some good work, a new stage of life will often bring the need for support again.

Priscilla now recognizes that getting married and having children, while joyful events in themselves, were also major psychological shifts that she couldn't cope with on her own. Even after therapy and then traveling well for a season, she needed help to navigate these good changes in life. I too have intermittently sought counseling to help for a season, including recently.

Owning and making this call is part of the responsibility of being in control of my life.

True recovery means giving yourself permission to ask for help whenever you need it.

Remember the Power of Speaking Thoughts Aloud

Trauma can feel like a swirling storm of noise. The feelings and memories make us anxious and sometimes panicky. Fears and small details are blown out of proportion. It's all too much for us to handle, and rather than deal with it carefully, we can feel rushed and act impulsively on those jumbled feelings or try to block them out. That's when we reach for something unhelpful, or even harmful.

I found it difficult to win the inner battle all by myself. It's no easy thing, and being guided through this process by an expert is part of what therapy is for. I've had to learn to pause and ask myself, "Why am I feeling this?" In fact, I often need to speak it aloud. Saying it out loud brings clarity in itself and helps us hear and understand what we are experiencing. It reduces and clarifies complex thoughts.

Talking out my feelings, including my worries, frustrations, fears, and even trivial things, has been a crucial strategy as I've taken back control of my mind. Priscilla and I agree that speaking our feelings aloud, no matter how trivial, is the single most empowering daily practice we know. Sometimes it brings surprising tears as I realize I was feeling very deeply about something that I had been minimizing in my mind. Other times things just make sense when spoken aloud: they're reduced to a proportionate size and become manageable.

Another reason speaking aloud is helpful is that it helps dispel the mental myths that pop into our heads, especially when we are tired. Priscilla struggles with the repeated line, "You will always be messed up"—which is clearly false, given the life she is leading and the recovery that has occurred and continues to occur. Sometimes she can win the mental battle internally, but sometimes it takes saying it out loud to dispel this lie. When we speak them aloud, mental myths are exposed to the scrutiny of reality.

Be Prepared for Ongoing Triggers and Flashbacks

We spoke about triggers in chapter two: the moment when something around us, even a tiny detail, sparks a traumatic memory or flashback. Our capacity to deal with mental triggers does increase as we become stronger over time, especially as we slowly come to appreciate that we are the masters of our own inner world. This is not to diminish the lordship of Jesus Christ over our lives; rather, it is to affirm that Christ gives us strength to "take every thought captive," as the apostle Paul puts it (2 Corinthians 10:5). Though images and feelings do still come out of the blue, our inner strength helps us manage them better over time. Our flashbacks tend to be more short-lived and don't quite wipe us out like they once did. That said, this battle is indeed a long one, and triggers can still come at the strangest moments. Priscilla and I have learned some strategies.

First, acknowledge it has happened. Don't deny it or try and squash it down. This is where speaking aloud can be helpful. Saying "I've just had a flashback" is often enough. Second, choose not to obsess over it. Unless you are actually in a counseling session, this is not the time to explore your memories. You are in control, and you can determine when this happens. And third, do something practical to distract yourself. Often a physical action works best, such as walking outside, turning on the television, picking up a guitar, talking to someone, or making a coffee. Your triggers are the past trying to hijack the present, and moving physically helps reconnect us with the present reality. This is also the case with disturbing dreams: if I wake up from one, I never just lay there hoping to get past it. Rather, I get up, turn on a light, go to the bathroom, get a drink, or read for a few minutes before going back to sleep. If you have a partner, it can be helpful to wake them for a brief conversation—perhaps on an entirely different topic—and a prayer.

Take Your Time with Sex

Sex can be an automatic trigger for survivors and can prompt vivid flashbacks. Indeed it can be the ultimate trigger for some. Many survivors find it a long-term struggle to separate adult sex from their past abuse experiences. Some find it almost impossible to think about.

So sex must be approached with the ultimate patience and care. It's a particularly tender and vulnerable area for recovery and healing, and requires kindness and understanding from our partner. Survivors must also be kind to themselves and give themselves time.

While this area is a complex one, a consistent principle applies: the survivor needs to feel safe and to have control in the situation, without any feelings of guilt or obligation. As with other flashbacks, speaking aloud and bringing yourself back to the present may be helpful. But this is not an easy road, and it can't be rushed. Each survivor is a different person, and may respond to sex in different ways.

It is crucial that there is growing trust between couples, shown in vulnerable mutual sharing and careful, nonjudgmental listening. Partners must demonstrate patience and love. There may be extended periods without sex.

It's a journey that must be made together. Remember, even couples who aren't survivors of sexual abuse experience tension in this area. Be kind to one another. A good overall exploration of the nature of sexuality is Debra Hirsch's book *Redeeming Sex*.

Be Careful with Coping Devices

Because of the chaotic stress survivors feel, we are particularly susceptible to things that seem to help us escape or feel in control. In chapter two I noted that abuse survivors are statistically more likely to abuse substances in ways that can do long-term damage. We must recognize the capacity of these escape mechanisms to control and damage us. We can easily form compulsive habits that provide a short-term feeling of freedom but that are in fact a mirage and lead to long-term bondage. I can still sense that addictive tendency in myself today. I smoked for many years, and when I finally decided to give it up, it was incredibly difficult—not only physically but psychologically. I was so reliant on the habit of finding peace by sitting and smoking alone.

The deep work of recovery can lessen the trauma beneath the pain we seek to escape as we slowly discover and explore the reasons we rely on these activities. But this is long-term work. In the meantime, we can take intermediate steps to recognize this tendency and experiment with activities that are less damaging.

For example, we can find alternative activities that produce serotonin in our brains, such as exercise. We can calm the noise in
our heads through meditation or breathing exercises.

Slowly but surely, our activities must shift from destructive
coping mechanisms to creative activities, enjoyed for their
own sake.

Determine to Learn Enjoyment

We mostly look for coping devices to numb us, but I invite you
to try and move toward other sensations that evoke pleasure. In
the midst of the complex thoughts and feelings, discover the
pleasures of the tangible world around you: the smell of a wood
fire, the feeling of carpet under bare feet, the taste of fresh bread.

Believe it or not, pleasure is one of the most necessary elements
of coping with trauma. Survivors of childhood trauma need to
learn to enjoy things. Most people learn to play when they are
children—that's what a free and healthy childhood is all about.
But survivors of childhood trauma spend their childhoods learning
to survive. They missed the crucial, carefree times of childhood.
Their instinct is to bunker down and manage danger, and they see
enjoyment as suspicious or indulgence or just unknown.

For some survivors of abuse, anything that isn't a struggle
doesn't seem quite right. In my case, this trajectory was set up
by my self-imposed obligation to forgive prematurely. I had
become so used to struggling that I was suspicious of anything
that came easily.

This pattern sabotages various areas of our lives. One example
is work. We may not feel we've done a proper day's work until we
are dog tired, so we work longer and harder. If we've enjoyed the

day, we might feel guilty about having a job that's too easy. Our inner barometer for proper enjoyment is broken. We need to learn that we were created for pleasure. Life, work, and relationships involve pleasure in themselves, without exhaustion or struggle.

Related to this, the loss of carefree play as children can also be accompanied by missing out of discovery of passions and interests through teenage years and beyond.

As we do the work of recovery, we gradually discover layers to ourselves that we have never explored, or even known. Priscilla in particular feels much freer in her forties than she ever has before. She's found in herself the desire to do things she has never done before. Just recently, while reading a magazine about artists, she realized that she has a quiet passion to paint. Having spent her life surviving, such a desire had never been given attention. The very thought of it felt like a ridiculous indulgence.

Talk to Just a Few Close Friends

We all need friends, but I've found it is important for survivors to cultivate a couple of very close friendships with people who understand the complexity of our experience and with whom we've shared far more than with others. It does not mean that these people are merely a support for us. True friendship is mutual. But survivors need friends who can sit with us in whatever stage we find ourselves in.

This does not mean we only talk about abuse—far from it. Rather, the shared understanding informs the depth of the friendship. C. S. Lewis said of friendship, "This does not mean that we are to be perpetually solemn. We must play. But our merriment must be of that kind (and it is, in fact, the merriest kind) which exists between people who have, from the outset, taken each other seriously."

Having one or two close friends who understand our journey is important. Don't make the circle too wide, or you might feel the obligation to be always updating people about vulnerable issues. Some survivors feel the need to go from person to person in an ever-lengthening line, relaying their story over and over. I advise against this. It won't lead to deeper growth or deeper relationships. That level of vulnerability and trust should not be spread too widely. It's often a symptom of not being deeply connected with ourselves, with the result that we look for meaning in affirmation from other people. We should recognize this inclination and talk about it with our therapists or counselors.

As Christian leaders, we can facilitate supportive groups as they emerge. If we want to take a hand in facilitating a support group, my advice is to enlist the help of someone with experience and training in this area. Much will depend on the level of the participants' recovery—and naturally, confidentiality is an important factor. We should do our best, in any case, to ensure that survivors are not journeying alone, and do what we can to connect them with a supporting small community. They don't even necessarily need to connect to an abuse support group—just an unconditionally loving cluster of people who understand brokenness.

Sleep and Exercise Are Your Friends

It's taken me a while to learn what a good friend sleep is—or, more to the point, how much harder it is to manage mental triggers when I'm tired. These days I'm addicted to getting to bed early, knowing how much more in control I feel with several nights of deep sleep in a row. Our sleep patterns, of course, will vary in different seasons of our life, and everyone is different. But getting to bed early helps me skip the mental triggers that can come late at night, when things feel insurmountable and getting to sleep at all can become a battle in itself.

Exercise too has several benefits. Getting out for a run, bicycle ride, or even long walk releases endorphins and can help bring a new mindset by changing our physical context. Exercise also, of course, helps us sleep better.

Identify Physical Sanctuaries

Survivors of trauma usually have incredibly noisy, anxious, and chaotic inner worlds. Often their greatest longing is for inner peace. This is why sanctuaries are important. Our therapist will often help us locate safe places to go to find sanctuary when our feelings overwhelm us. For many people, this will include being in our bed at home. But we need other places as well, perhaps near work and so forth.

There's a strong connection between our inner world and our physical location. Priscilla and I have found it important to recognize the physical locations and environments we find safe, and to plan regular times to be in them. But we've also come to see that this works differently for both of us. For example, Priscilla loves the beach. Being in or near the ocean is enormously calming for her. She loves to swim, feel the sand, and look out toward the horizon. She feels connected with herself and alive. Often, if her day has been overwhelming and her inner world is depleted, she'll drive home via the beach and find sanctuary there for a while. For my part, I spent countless hours alone

sitting in my car at Brighton Beach near Adelaide during the
winter, watching the waves. It felt spacious and safe, reading in
the car in winter.

This may seem a trivial matter. What does the beach have to
do with sexual abuse? But it's important because trauma survivors have a heightened sense of safety and a more finely tuned
sense of their physical environment. In the midst of this long-
term battle, bringing our psychological world into order and
calm is a great help.

Priscilla loves the open spaces of the rural outdoors, whereas,
depending on my mindset, I can sometimes find the open spaces
empty and strangely threatening. My mind tends to spin busily.
I like to be distracted and occupied with new, interesting information. Faced with nothing but scenery, it takes me a while to
slow down and relax. I much prefer urban environments,
especially cities. My preferred sanctuary is a big city. I love the
solitude, the anonymous freedom, and the endless physical
information. Musician Kim Gordon, from the band Sonic
Youth, makes this point about life in New York: "If you're at all
anxious," she writes, "the city acts out your anxiety for you,
leaving you feeling strangely peaceful." That's what I often feel—
the chaos of the city absorbs my anxiety and makes me feel calm
and connected with myself. But I recognize that unless I find
some quieter space, this too can become a distraction.

One practical way a Christian leader can help survivors is
to recognize that from time to time, even during a church
service, a survivor may need to leave to find a safe space. You
can also help by unassumingly identifying a quiet room where
a survivor can go to be alone on the church property. As always,

the choice is theirs, and it's not something that should be made known widely.

Identify Mental Sanctuaries Too

It's fascinating to see the various kinds of art that different survivors are drawn to. I've noticed, for example, a difference between the novels I prefer and the novels Priscilla prefers. Priscilla's favorite novels are set in the rural or natural environments. She loves authors like Tim Winton, with his long descriptions of the space, tranquility, and details of the natural world. I gravitate toward urban novels, such as the novels of Paul Auster, which are often set in Brooklyn.

This brings us to the fascinating idea of inner sanctuaries—places we can go in our minds to help calm us. I've mentioned that meditation and rehearsed visualization of safe spaces can be a real asset when we are struggling to cope. Similarly, films, music, and books offer a controlled world to escape into. In a 2001 article in *Harpers Magazine*, novelist Jonathan Franzen refers to the kinds of people who are drawn to certain novels—and I think his point also transfers to certain television shows and films. He cites a study by Shirley Brice Heath, a linguistic anthropologist and English professor at Stanford University, who analyzed people who read substantive works of fiction. She found that many had reading modeled to them when they were young by their parents or a significant peer. But she also found a second kind of reader:

> There's the social isolate—the child who from an early age felt very different from everyone around him. What happens is

they take that sense of being different into an imaginary world. But that world, then, is a world you can't share with the people around you—because it's imaginary. And so the important dialogue in your life is with the authors of the books you read. They aren't present, they become your community.

Some survivors will identify with this feeling of displacement from the world around them. They find company in the world of imagination. Franzen then makes an important distinction between *displaced* sociability and *anti*-sociability. These readers aren't antisocial—indeed, sometimes they can be hypersocial. "It's just that at some point you'll begin to feel a gnawing, almost remorseful need to be alone and do some reading—to reconnect with that community." That's an inner sanctuary—a secret world where we feel normal. At school I would often spend my lunch break in the library reading. I wasn't studying at all, just reading—anything: novels, magazines, or even Tintin. It felt quiet, safe, and interesting. For some reason I preferred it to the hustle and bustle of the playground.

Franzen then suggests some people are drawn to the darkness and unpredictability of life, as presented through the articulate beauty and clarity of literature. Having this tragic realism presented in a book is powerful for them. "The formal aesthetic rendering of the human plight can be . . . redemptive." He notes that readers generally feel that reading actually "makes them a better person." Not in a self-help way, but (to quote Heath again), "Reading serious literature impinges on the embedded circumstances in people's lives in such a way that they have to deal with them. And, in so dealing, they come to see themselves as deeper and more capable of handling their inability to have a totally predictable life."

People who have suffered trauma can actually be more drawn to find sanctuary in certain kinds of novels. I think there is truth in this, though I know that the predictability of some films and novels can also be deeply reassuring.

There is, however, an enormous amount of trauma presented in television series and films. I've found as the years go by that I've lost my taste for a certain level of violence or trauma on screen. Priscilla and I have found that at times, one or the other of us would rather watch something safe and predictable, while at other times that feels too unrealistic and we look for something more engaging. Some people have a favorite series that they find comfort in watching, a familiar world where they can rest their mind. Of course this is only a respite, a periodic escape. We cannot live in these places, and they cannot become a permanent escape. Ultimately, learning strategies to quiet our minds and be present with ourselves will be the most help.

Perhaps the healthiest sanctuary can be the world of the Bible, where we encounter not only the Psalms, which we've noted, but also the person of Jesus in the Gospels. We hear his voice, and we see him engaging tenderly with people, touching and healing the outcasts, talking to them and giving them dignity. All through the Bible we encounter God's Word speaking to our heads and our hearts. One of the beauties of the Bible is its vivid honesty about the realities of life, along with the deep assurance of the love of God. There is nothing superficial in the Bible, but there is plenty of comfort. I've found that reading passages and then sitting quietly and meditating on them becomes a kind of prayer, honest and short. During times of pain, the Bible has been my regular refuge.

Discover the Mysterious Power of Duende in Art

The phenomenon of *duende* was first noted by the Spanish poet Frederico García Lorca. In his 1933 lecture "The Theory and Play of Duende," he described *duende* as "a mysterious force that everyone feels and no philosopher has explained." It is a deep connection with true sadness, the more profound aches of humanity—a connection that is hard to describe. García Lorca recalls an old guitar *maestro* who said: "The *duende* is not in the throat: the *duende* surges up, inside, from the soles of the feet. . . . Meaning it's not a question of skill, but of a style that's truly alive: meaning it's in the veins: meaning, it's of the most ancient culture of immediate creation."

Some artists—painters, poets, musicians, dancers, and writers—determine to work with the possibility of "dark sounds," which are the "mystery, the roots that cling to the mire that we all know, that we all ignore, but from which comes the very substance of art." Those dark sounds are the true sadness that gives rise to true beauty. García Lorca goes on, "The *duende* loves the edge, the wound, and draws close to places where forms fuse in a yearning beyond visible expression."

What García Lorca is describing is what people in pain feel when a piece of art speaks profoundly to their experience. It is the feeling of being understood—the deeply cathartic feeling of realizing that *someone knows*. In that moment, the art is speaking not just to us but for us. I had one such moment when I saw the film *Inside Out*. However, I realize now that I've sought *duende* for years without realizing it. The singer/songwriter Nick Cave further elaborated on García Lorca's concepts:

> All love songs must contain *duende*. For the love song is never truly happy. It must first embrace the potential for pain. Those songs that speak of love without having within their lines an ache or a sigh are not love songs at all, but rather hate song disguised as love songs, and are not to be trusted. These songs deny us our humanness and our God-given right to be sad, and the airwaves are littered with them. The love song must resonate with the susurration of sorrow, the tintinnabulation of grief. The writer who refuses to explore the darker regions of the heart will never be able to write convincingly about the wonder, the magic and the joy of love. . . . So within the fabric of the love song, within its melody, its lyric, one must sense an acknowledgement of its capacity for suffering.

Cave goes on to reference the lament psalms as perfect examples of *duende*: songs of love that know the reality of suffering. This is why Cave can say that all true love songs not only have sadness at their core but also are songs of longing, ultimately for God: "For the love song is the light of God, deep down, blasting through our wounds."

Cave mentions several musicians as examples, including Bob Dylan, Van Morrison, Tom Waits, PJ Harvey, and Neil Young. But the master of the *duende* is probably Leonard Cohen. His famous song "Hallelujah" is the classic example—a love song that contains the ache of spiritual yearning and surrender. No wonder it's been covered so many times. People resonate deeply with its sweet and hopeful sadness. Consider also Cohen's song "Anthem":

Ring the bells that still can ring
Forget your perfect offering
There is a crack, a crack in everything
That's how the light gets in.

As a survivor of extreme trauma who feels cracked, broken, and hurt, these words speak deeply to me. I am comforted and even thrilled by them. They orient my heart toward God, who sees me and meets me in the darkness.

Explore the Christian Contemplative Tradition

I wasn't a big reader of contemplative literature until a friend, Shirley, gave me a book by Jean Vanier called *The Broken Body*—and then, later, Priscilla gave me the same book for my birthday. Jean Vanier founded L'Arche, a network of communities for people with developmental disabilities and those who assist them. He writes beautifully about the brokenness of the world.

Today we are seeing the birth of a newly fragile humanity:
Lonely, bewildered,
Lacking references and a sense of belonging:
Feeling empty,
But finding nothing to fill the emptiness.

Vanier walks through the brokenness of humanity and invites us to embark on a journey toward wholeness, with the narrative of Jesus at the core. It's an easy read, and perfect for an anxious mind. Many times I've been thankful to have it with me. After reading Vanier, I discovered other contemplative writers such as Henri Nouwen, who also writes beautifully about brokenness and wholeness.

The "dark night of the soul" is a phrase we often use to describe difficult times, but not many people know where it originally comes from. It's the name of a poem by the sixteenth-century Spanish mystic St. John of the Cross.

> O guiding dark of night!
> O dark of night more darling than the dawn!
> O night that can unite
> A lover and loved one,
> A lover and loved one moved in unison.

The poem describes the journey of the soul into union with God. It gives voice to the painful seasons that mark our journey toward spiritual maturity. The poem has given its name to a variety of profound spiritual or physical crises, even outside the Christian tradition. The notion of the "dark night of the soul" perfectly names our experiences of grief, doubt, pain, and suffering.

St. John of the Cross wrote from personal experience. He once spent nine months imprisoned in a small cell, enduring lashings, and with only water, bread, and scraps of fish to eat, when he was caught up in the political and religious conflicts of his time. It's not easy to write about dark nights of the soul from personal experience. It must have traumatized him.

The poem teaches us that just because we're going through suffering and darkness doesn't mean we're far from the will of God. It doesn't mean we're lost or forgotten. The poem speaks of the darkness ultimately becoming "more darling than the dawn," since it has led us to the love of God. "O night that can unite / A lover and loved one." The dark night is not a sign of chaos. In the end, it facilitates the union of the soul with God.

Another contemplative writer who has been helpful for me is Julian of Norwich. Her fourteenth-century book *Revelations of Divine Love* is said to be the first book ever published in the English language written by a woman. It is a compendium of visions and reflections on the hope of God in the midst of adversity.

Those who have suffered know that God is always with them, even in the dark valleys. As Christian leaders, we can incorporate the best of the Christian contemplative tradition into our preaching, or even our worship.

Seek Simplicity and Complexity

Despite having completed two degrees, Priscilla has never felt like a natural student. Every essay is hard work. But part of what has made Christianity compelling to her is its depth and complexity, which resonates with her experience of life. She found that she could not stand Christian platitudes, and had to go and search the truth for herself. She had to have intelligent conversations about faith. For her, listening to substantial, nuanced teaching and preaching is bliss. There's something about sitting in the complexity that brings peace.

This is a common experience for many people at some point during their recovery. Some find immersion in complex ideas to be a religious experience. Priscilla says, "My own inner complexity feels welcome, and resonates with the complexity of great theology. Even though I don't fully understand, I feel God's closeness and presence." This isn't about intelligence; it's about a way of being in the world.

Counterintuitive to this is our natural longing for a simpler life. As much as we may welcome complexity at times, we cope best when we keep the structure of our lives simple. That means giving ourselves plenty of space and time. Life offers enough events, relationships, and chaos all by itself. Survivors do well to leave themselves extra margins. Priscilla and I know that we need more time than others to recreate. That means keeping good boundaries and resisting the obligation to be busy according to the timetable of modern life. We will always be somewhat more susceptible to stress than we think. This is not to place limits on what we can do with our lives, but to be wise about the number of things we can take on at once.

Complexity and simplicity come from the habits and patterns of our lives. We need the simple reassurance of repeated activities in our days and weeks. As Christians leaders, we should recognize this dynamic as we preach. There should be an elegant simplicity to our sermons, but we shouldn't be afraid of complex ideas. Survivors can be empowered by the richness of ambiguity and nuance.

Remember That Survivors Have Both More and Less Resilience

Survivors have an interesting relationship with resilience. Our trauma experience makes us both more and less resilient. Many survivors feel more ready to handle a dire emergency than a dinner party. Having lived through trauma, we may be more prepared for significant disasters or emergencies than other people. We can be shockproof to dire situations that leave other people frozen, and we are used to living in a constant state of alertness. This phenomenon is evident, for example, in soldiers returning from war.

The trouble is, of course, that this constant alertness ultimately drains our bodies. We may be ready in the event of a disaster, but lost otherwise. This can make us far less resilient in the ordinary requirements of life.

We develop true resilience by doing the vulnerable inner work of guided recovery. As we face these complex matters and slowly become whole, we will build deep inner resources. All human beings are fragile, but we do not internalize the reality that we are all fragile until we experience suffering. Suffering awakens to us to the fragility of life. We discover the hard-won secrets of real hope. In the long run, having been through trauma and kept walking, we're no longer scared of the worst thing happening. That is, our ongoing choice to seek the help we need and to persist with our journey of recovery is an indication of profound resilience.

There has been some recent discussion about the way stressful childhoods shape our adult lives. The traumatic stress from an experience such as sexual abuse can result in "hostile attribution bias," an overdeveloped awareness of potential threats. Hyper-vigilant parenting is just one expression of this. But some recent research seeks to identify the flipside of this. Is there a potential upside to developing such coping mechanisms? These might include greater perceptiveness in reading people, a heightened ability to detect danger, and an advanced ability to adapt to threatening situations. Certainly Priscilla and I can relate to these traits. I do feel nervous about celebrating them, though, because of the potential for childhood stress to be minimized. These traits are overdeveloped for a tragic reason, after all, and sensitivity to danger can be stressful. So none of this is to affirm childhood stress, much less trauma from abuse. But as we explore the impact of trauma on our lives and identify the places where redemption is at work, we can affirm that the creative ways we have adapted to survive can have an upside too.

In this we can become a great gift to others who are suffering in our communities. We can be helpful truth-tellers, more acutely aware of the emptiness of the myths and idols our culture distracts itself with. Even so, the little things can still throw us. Making it through small talk can take all the strength we can muster. I have come to accept that I am both resilient and fragile—but my fragility is never the final word.

Relish the Wonder of Weeping

Consider the wonderful phenomenon of tears. Recovery often involves crying, and I've shared a few times in this book when tears have filled my eyes. What did they accomplish?

Crying is a mystery. It feels strangely wonderful, even as we feel awful. While often prompted by sadness, it actually brings a welcome, understated sweetness. It doesn't immediately resolve things—unless resisting the truth of our feelings is a problem, which it often is. But tears are the natural guests of extreme circumstances, a strange condolence. They say the perfect thing every time. Of course some people, in the face of grief or deep sadness, cry every single day. And some friends of mine say they haven't cried for years. We don't go looking for it, and it can be avoided. And then, of course, it can catch us unexpectedly, almost like a kind of confession. "Yes," the tears admit, "I am hurting."

Crying is an open, vulnerable act. We can't pretend much during a real cry. We feel the inertia of release, of letting go. While we tend to equate it with our tears, crying actually seems to come from the chest, with deep breathing. After a cry, we exhale and often remain strangely still. It's a special kind of space, those few seconds, as we rejoin real time.

Crying with others is also incredibly precious. The mutual expression binds us together beyond words, carving out a space where the truly important, human things are in the center. For a moment, everything superficial falls away. Sometimes this is profoundly important, when tears accompany the most horrific events. They seem to be prompted by matters of extreme resonance, sometimes due to our tenderness and other times because of the sheer significance of the circumstances, whether exhilaratingly joyful or devastatingly sad.

Crying can be incredibly cathartic, which means it brings psychological clarity through the cleansing experience of expressing strong emotions. Often this happens through art. Art gives physical expression to our psychological states, particularly when it touches on our deepest values and longings. Novels, films, music, drama, dance, and paintings can skillfully speak to us in ways that prompt tears. And these can be a real gift, especially if they just happen to catch us at the right moment.

In Ecclesiastes we read, "For everything there is a season, and a time for every matter under heaven . . . a time to weep, and a time to laugh" (Ecclesiastes 3:1, 4). We're also told that at the death of Lazarus, "Jesus wept" (John 11:35). Jesus cried, and so do we.

Choose Life

At the beginning of this chapter, Priscilla shared about a particular moment in her journey when she decided to "choose life"—when she realized that she wanted to make life-giving choices for herself and wanted a path that would help her become whole.

For some, just reading this book may have been an enormously courageous step. But wherever you are on the journey of recovery, remember that you don't have to do it on your own. You have the right and the power to ask for help whenever you're ready. You have the right to heal and to become whole. You are already a survivor—you are already on the way. The God of all comfort, justice, love, and compassion sees you, knows you, and loves you.

Jesus said, "The thief comes only to steal and kill and destroy. I came that they may have life, and have it abundantly" (John 10:10). Wherever we are on our journeys of life, including the journeys of recovery and healing, we can make choices about the paths ahead. We can choose life, and go on doing so, because Jesus, the author of life, has come. At the cross Jesus entered into the depths of trauma and then death, and then rose again victoriously. He said, "Come to me, all you that are weary and are carrying heavy burdens, and I will give you rest" (Matthew 11:28).

Look to Jesus, rest in him, and let him help you walk the journey to come.

ACKNOWLEDGMENTS

I'm very grateful to the many people who have contributed to this book with encouragement, friendship, love, advice, expertise, wisdom, and support.

To David McGregor, Bob Kempe, John Ledson, Graham Humphris, Craig Bailey, Sharonne Price, Mark Sayers, Alan and Debra Hirsch, Michael Frost, Dan Kimball, John Smith, David Fuller, Shirley Osborn, Davin Hood, Matthew Johnson, Brady Haran, Duncan Handley, Daniel Norris, Patricia Benjamin, Chris and Jess Moerman, and the CPR guys: John Manning, Nick Greer, Cameron Byson, and Pete Moncrieff.

To Andrew Dutney, John Capper, Liz Boase, Tanya Wittwer, Deidre Palmer, and Phil Carr for reading the manuscript, or parts thereof. To the faculty and staff, past and present, of Uniting College for Leadership and Theology; the Adelaide College of Divinity; and to the South Australian Presbytery and Synod of the Uniting Church in Australia.

Also to Alan Jenkins, Tanja Stojadinovic, the Dulwich Centre, Jussey Verco, Linda Vinall, and Vince Vitale for resources and expertise.

Thanks to my editors, Helen Lee, Cindy Bunch, and Ethan McCarthy, for their wisdom and skill.

To my mother, Dawn Hein, and my late father, Geert.

Especially to the kind and courageous Priscilla, who has put so much into this book.

And above all to God, who is faithful.

Soli Deo Gloria

NOTES

Introduction

3   *as many as half of the incidents are not reported*: This figure is based on
a wide range of studies. There is a growing body of research on the
prevalence of abuse, but studies differ in method and scope due to the
complexity of the subject. So the US Center for Disease Control and
Prevention states one in four females and one in six males were abused
as children (www.cdc.gov/violenceprevention/acestudy/about.html),
while a 2011 meta-analysis of global prevalence figures found that 19.7
percent of females and 8.8 percent of males reported a history of child
sexual abuse (Marije Stoltenborgh, Marinus H. Van Ljzendoorn,
Eveline M. Euser, and Marian J. Bakermans-Kranenburg, "A Global
Perspective on Child Sexual Abuse: Misanalysis of Prevalence Around
the World," *Child Maltreatment* 16, no. 2 [May 2011]: 79-101). The
Australian government resource sheet states that up to 26.8 percent
of females and 12 percent of males have been abused (Kate Rosier, *The
Prevalence of Child Abuse and Neglect*, Australian Institute of Family
Studies, updated April 2017, https://aifs.gov.au/cfca/publications
/prevalence-child-abuse-and-neglect).

   Because abuse is secretive, all agree that a significant number of occurrences go unreported (some even say the majority), so that even formal
prevalence studies should be considered conservative. For example, a 2009
meta-analysis of international studies found that 7.9 percent of men and
19.7 percent of women have been sexually abused, yet concluded, "This
method of study inevitably underestimates the extent of the problem, and
by no means does an incidence rate establish the real occurrence of child
sexual abuse" (Noemi Pereda, Georgina Guilerab, Maria Fornsa, and
Juana Gómez-Benito, "The Prevalence of Child Sexual Abuse in Community and Student Samples: A Meta-analysis," *Clinical Psychology
Review* 29, no. 4 [June 2009]: 328-38).

1 A Safe Place

13   *standards set by state authorities and denominational bodies*: One example is the Uniting Church in Australia National Child Safe Policy
Framework (2017), http://uca.org.au/national-child-safety-policy
-framework.

21   *Somehow, I've always known*: *Return of the Jedi*, directed by Richard Marquand (San Francisco: Lucasfilm, 1983).

2 Why Abuse Hurts

29   *Traumatic experiences can affect*: Child Welfare Information Gateway, "Understanding the Effects of Maltreatment on Brain Development," US Department of Health and Human Services, Children's Bureau, April 2015. www.childwelfare.gov/pubs/issue-briefs/brain-development.

30   *This biology plays out in our behavior*: Judy Cashmore and Rita Shackel, "The Long-Term Effects of Sexual Abuse," Child Family Community Australia, paper no. 11 (January 2013), aifs.gov.au/cfca/publications/long-term-effects-child-sexual-abuse.

    In 1998, Dr. Vincent Felitti and his team: Vincent Felitti et al., "Relationship of Childhood Abuse and Household Dysfunction to Many of the Leading Causes of Death in Adults," *American Journal of Preventive Medicine* 14, no. 4 (May 1998): 245-58.

    is cited in a report by the World Health Organization: Alexander Butchart and Alison Phinney Harvey, *Preventing Child Maltreatment: A Guide to Taking Action and Generating Evidence*, World Health Organization and International Society for Prevention of Child Abuse and Neglect (2006), apps.who.int/iris/bitstream/10665/43499/1/9241594365_eng.pdf.

31   *people of the clearest intellect*: Josef Breuer and Sigmund Freud, "Studies on Hysteria" (1893–1895), in *Standard Edition of the Complete Psychological Works of Sigmund Freud*, vol. 2, trans. J. Strachey (London: Hogarth Press, 1973–1974), 13.

32   *I therefore put forward the thesis*: Sigmund Freud, "The Aetiology of Hysteria" (1896), in *Standard Edition*, vol. 3, trans. J. Strachey (London: Hogarth Press, 1962), 203.

    Our children are far more often exposed: Gerald N. Izenberg, "Seduced and Abandoned: The Rise and Fall of Freud's Seduction Theory," in *The Cambridge Companion to Freud*, ed. Jerome Neu (Cambridge: Cambridge University Press, 1991), 25-43.

33   *"The Battered Child Syndrome"*: C. Henry Kempe et al., "The Battered Child Syndrome," *Journal of the American Medical Association* 181 (July 7, 1962): 17-24.

    the same as the effect of trauma on survivors of war: Ibid., 32.

33   *accepted by all experts in the field*: Arthur Green, "Child Sexual Abuse: Immediate, and Long Term Effects and Intervention," *Journal of the American Academy of Child & Adolescent Psychiatry* 32, no. 5 (1993): 890-902.

34   *Human beings are meaning-making creatures*: Bessel Van Der Kolk, Onno Van Der Hart, and Charles R. Marmar, "Dissociation and Information Processing in Posttraumatic Stress Disorder," in *Traumatic Stress: The Effects of Overwhelming Experience on Mind, Body, and Society*, ed. Bessel Van Der Kolk et al. (New York: Guilford Press, 1996), 304.

36   *immature system of psychological defenses*: Judith Herman, *Trauma and Recovery: The Aftermath of Violence—From Domestic Abuse to Political Terror* (New York: Basic Books, 1997), 96. In this section I have leaned significantly on Herman, who stands tall in this field and whose work in this area has been groundbreaking and insightful.

      [Childhood abuse] fosters the development: Ibid., 96.

37   *The assumption of badness*: J. H. Beitchman, K. J. Zucker, J. E. Hood, G. A. daCosta, and D. Akman, "A Review of the Short-Term Effects of Child Sexual Abuse," in *Child Abuse & Neglect* 15, no. 4 (1991): 537-56.

41   *a dreadful feeling that psychiatrists call 'dysphoria'*: Herman, *Trauma and Recovery*, 108.

42   *affecting our innermost sensations*: Bessel Van Der Kolk, *The Body Keeps the Score: Brain, Mind, and Body in the Healing of Trauma* (London: Penguin, 2014), 21.

48   *It is not unusual for young survivors to do things*: Jennifer Tebbutt et al., "Five Years After Child Sexual Abuse: Persisting Dysfunction and Problems of Prediction," *Journal of the American Academy of Child & Adolescent Psychiatry* 36, no. 3 (March 1997): 330-39.

49   *traumatic events overwhelm the ordinary symptoms*: Herman, *Trauma and Recovery*, 33.

      hyperarousal, intrusion, and constriction: Ibid., 35-47.

3 Breaking the Power of Secrets

56   *allowed to narrate freely*: Families SA, *Child-Safe Environments: Reporting Child Abuse & Neglect Participant Workbook and Information for Organizations*, Department for Education and Child Development, Government of South Australia (2013).

56   *ask general, nonthreatening questions*: Ibid.

59   *the first principle of the recovery*: Judith Herman, *Trauma and Recovery: The Aftermath of Violence—From Domestic Abuse to Political Terror* (New York: Basic Books, 1997), 133.

67   *the deep sense that you are unacceptable*: Edward T. Welch, *Shame Interrupted: How God Lifts the Pain of Worthlessness and Rejection* (Greensboro, NC: New Growth Press, 2012), 2.

     You feel like an outcast: Ibid., 27.

68   *Empirical studies indicate*: For example, Sigrun Sigurdardottir, Sigridur Halldorsdottir, and Soley S. Bender, "Deep and Almost Unbearable Suffering: Consequences of Child Sexual Abuse for Men's Health and Well-Being," *Scandinavian Journal of Caring Sciences* 26, no. 4 (December 2012): 688-97.

     Research indicates that talking to someone: Ibid.

69   *Contrary to the popular notion*: Herman, *Trauma and Recovery*, 114.

     This is the largest prospective study: James R. P. Ogloff, Margaret C. Cutajar, Emily Mann, and Paul Mullen, "Child Sexual Abuse and Subsequent Offending and Victimisation: A 45 Year Follow-up Study," *Trends and Issues in Crime and Criminal Justice* 440 (June 2012).

     Some suggest the experience of victimisation: Email to the author, June 9, 2017.

4 What Does Recovery Look Like?

80   *the action or process of regaining possession*: *Concise Oxford English Dictionary*, 11th ed. (Oxford: Oxford University Press, 2008).

     This truth cannot be over-emphasized: Dan B. Allender, *The Wounded Heart: Hope for Adult Victims of Childhood Sexual Abuse* (Colorado Springs, CO: NavPress, 1990), 190.

     the will to extend one's self: M. Scott Peck, *The Road Less Traveled: A New Psychology of Love, Traditional Values and Spiritual Growth* (London: Arrow Books, 1983), 81.

81   *When we extend ourselves*: Ibid., 131.

82   *Her three stages are as follows*: Judith Herman, *Trauma and Recovery: The Aftermath of Violence—From Domestic Abuse to Political Terror* (New York: Basic Books, 1997). These are Herman's categories, but the explanations are in my words.

82   *from unpredictable danger to reliable safety*: Ibid., 155.

83   *their overview is worth quoting in full*: Ellen Bass and Laura Davis, *The Courage to Heal: A Guide for Women Survivors of Child Sexual Abuse*, 4th ed. (New York: CollinsLiving, 2008), 56-57.

85   *With this love comes a feeling of belonging*: Ibid., 169.

89   *Only through mourning everything*: Herman, *Trauma and Recovery*, 188.

     After many repetitions, the moment arrives: Ibid., 195.

5 Justice, Anger, and the Question of Forgiveness

95   *an important step on the path*: David Denborough, "Protected: Women's Outrage and the Pressure to Forgive: An Interview with Jussey Verco," *International Journal of Narrative Therapy & Community Work* 1 (2002): 23.

96   *Research indicates that this pressure*: See, for example, Alan Jenkins, Rob Hall, and Maxine Joy, "Forgiveness and Child Sexual Abuse: A Matrix of Meanings," *The International Journal of Narrative Therapy and Community Work* 1 (2002): 35-51. See also Sharon Lamb and Jeffrie G. Murphy, eds., *Before Forgiving: Cautionary Views of Forgiveness in Psychotherapy*, (New York: Oxford University Press, 2002).

     that she can transcend her rage: Judith Herman, *Trauma and Recovery: The Aftermath of Violence—From Domestic Abuse to Political Terror* (New York: Basic Books, 1997), 190.

97   *Experts specifically note that an obligated*: Jenkins, Hall, and Joy, "Forgiveness and Child Sexual Abuse."

     It requires the recognition of injustice: Karen Lebacqz, "Love Your Enemy: Sex, Power and Christian Ethics," in *Feminist Theological Ethics: A Reader*, ed. Lois K. Daly (Louisville: Westminster John Knox Press, 1994), 244-62 (here 253).

98   *Should we disregard such offenses?*: Miroslav Volf, *Free of Charge: Giving and Forgiving in a Culture Stripped of Grace* (Grand Rapids: Zondervan, 2005), 168.

99   *First, that human beings*: C. S. Lewis, *Mere Christianity* (New York: Macmillan, 1952), 18.

103 *backbone of healing*: Ellen Bass and Laura Davis, *The Courage to Heal: A Guide for Women Survivors of Child Sexual Abuse*, 3rd ed. (Santa Cruz, CA: HarperPerennial, 1994), 143.

103   *clears the way for self-acceptance*: Ibid.

      a greater freedom marked by discovering new meanings: Jenkins, Hall, and
      Joy, "Forgiveness and Child Sexual Abuse," 35.

104   *research indicates that playing out images*: Herman, *Trauma and Recovery*, 189.

      Revenge will not satisfy our anger: Ibid.

105   *My thesis that the practice*: Miroslav Volf, *Exclusion and Embrace: A
      Theological Exploration of Identity, Otherness, and Reconciliation* (Nash-
      ville: Abingdon Press, 1996), 304.

106   *gradually changes into a more powerful*: Herman, *Trauma and Recovery*, 189.

108   *Jenkins, Hall, and Joy suggest*: Jenkins, Hall, and Joy, "Forgiveness and
      Child Sexual Abuse," 35.

110   *Indeed, they may eventually reach*: Herman, *Trauma and Recovery*, 190.

111   *Eventually the time to forgive may come*: Volf, *Free of Charge*, 207.

6 Where Is God?

114   *As Christian leaders, it's important to recognize*: The distinction between the
      intellectual and emotional responses to the problem of evil is discussed
      in several places, including William Lane Craig, *Hard Questions, Real
      Answers* (Wheaton, IL: Crossway, 2003), 80.

116   *Of course I quite agree*: C. S. Lewis, *Mere Christianity* (New York: Mac-
      millan, 1952), 38.

117   *Alister McGrath advises against the temptation*: Alister McGrath, *Mere
      Apologetics: How to Help Seekers and Skeptics to Find Faith* (Grand
      Rapids: Baker Books, 2012), 161.

121   *My argument against God*: Lewis, *Mere Christianity*, 42.

122   *Unless we allow ultimate reality to be moral*: Lewis, *Christian Reflections*
      (Grand Rapids: Eerdmans, 1967), 70.

      clue to the meaning of the universe: Lewis, *Mere Christianity*, 15.

123   *If we ask why God created*: Richard Rice, "The Mystery of Suffering,"
      Update 2 (October 1986): 3, quoted in Stanley Hauerwas, *Naming the
      Silences: God, Medicine, and the Problem of Suffering* (Grand Rapids:
      Eerdmans, 1990), 73.

124   *If you have a God infinite and powerful enough*: Timothy Keller, *Walking with God Through Pain and Suffering* (London: Hodder and Stoughton, 2013), 99.

      God has willed his good in creatures: David Bentley Hart, *The Doors of the Sea: Where Was God in the Tsunami?* (Grand Rapids: Eerdmans, 2005), 82.

      He will therefore act: N. T. Wright, *Evil and the Justice of God* (London: SPCK, 2006), 73-74.

126   *We picture ourselves in this world*: Ravi Zacharias and Vince Vitale, *Why Suffering? Finding Meaning and Comfort When Life Doesn't Make Sense* (New York: FaithWords, 2014), 68.

      We often wish we could: Ibid., 71.

127   *a present and enduring object of God's love*: Ibid., 76.

7 A Broken Hallelujah

131   *Parker Palmer explains*: Parker Palmer, *Let Your Life Speak: Listening for the Voice of Vocation* (San Francisco: Jossey-Bass, 2000), 62.

132   *whatever comfort or counsel these people*: Ibid.

      simply stand respectfully at the edge: Ibid., 63.

      By standing respectfully and faithfully: Ibid., 64.

133   *neither avoids nor invades the soul's suffering*: Ibid.

      animated film Inside Out: *Inside Out*, directed by Pete Docter (Emeryville, CA: Pixar Animation Studios, 2015).

136   *the effusive expression of gratitude and praise*: Marianne Meye Thompson, "Reflections on Joy in the Bible," in *Joy and Human Flourishing: Essays on Theology, Culture, and the Good Life*, ed. Miroslav Volf and Justin E. Crisp (Minneapolis: Fortress, 2015), 38.

137   *the songs of Jesus*: Timothy Keller, *The Songs of Jesus: A Year of Daily Devotions in the Psalms* (New York: Viking Press, 2015).

      the Psalms have a unique place in the Bible: Bernhard W. Anderson (with Steven Bishop), *Out of the Depths: The Psalms Speak for Us Today*, 3rd ed. (Louisville: Westminster John Knox, 2000), ix (emphasis original).

138   *The psalmists, despite their intensity*: Interview with Matt Smethurst, "The Book Tim Keller's Read Every Month for 20 Years," The Gospel

Coalition, November 25, 2015, www.thegospelcoalition.org/article/book-tim-keller-read-every-month-20-years.

139 *On the one hand, we are to lay open our hearts*: J. Todd Billings, *Rejoicing in Lament: Wrestling with Incurable Cancer & Life in Christ* (Grand Rapids: Brazos Press, 2015), 43.

141 *when you listen to Adams's cover*: James K. A. Smith, "Liturgical Lessons from Ryan Adams's *1989*," *Fors Clavigera* (September 25, 2015), http://forsclavigera.blogspot.com.au/2015/09/liturgical-lessons-from-ryan-adams-1989.html.

143 *Lament gives a voice to suffering*: John Swinton, *Raging with Compassion: Pastoral Responses to the Problem of Evil* (Grand Rapids: Eerdmans, 2007), 107.

I guess I did my grieving for my father: Tom Doyle, "10 Years of Turmoil Inside U2," *Q Magazine*, October 10, 2002.

I waited patiently: U2, "40," *War*, Island Records, 1983.

144 *It included an invocation*: Elizabeth Boase and Steve Taylor, "Public Lament," in *Spiritual Complaint: The Theology and Practice of Lament*, ed. Miriam J. Bier and Tim Bulkeley (Eugene, OR: Pickwick, 2013), 205-27.

145 *Ah, I'd love to wear*: Johnny Cash, "Man in Black," *Man in Black*, Columbia Records, 1971.

146 *implement the victory of God*: N. T. Wright, *Evil and the Justice of God* (London: SPCK, 2006), 98.

147 *a community of care actually able to absorb evil*: Stanley Hauerwas, *God, Medicine, and the Problem of Suffering* (Grand Rapids: Eerdmans, 1990), 53.

149 *In keeping with the status of Israel's people*: Michael Trainor, *The Body of Jesus and Sexual Abuse: How the Gospel Passion Narratives Inform a Pastoral Response* (Northcote, VIC: Morning Star Publishing, 2014), 41.

151 *Only through weakness and pain*: Timothy Keller, *Walking with God Through Pain and Suffering* (London: Hodder and Stoughton, 2013), 51.

153 *Jesus suffers the full consequences of evil*: Wright, *Evil and the Justice of God*, 92.

155 *The New Testament invites us*: Ibid., 118.

8 Choosing Life

166   *This does not mean that we are to be perpetually solemn*: C. S. Lewis, *The Weight of Glory and Other Addresses* (New York: Macmillan, 1949), 46.

169   *If you're at all anxious*: Kim Gordon, *Girl in a Band* (New York: Harper-Collins, 2015), 226.

170   *novelist Jonathan Franzen refers to*: Jonathan Franzen, "Perchance to Dream: In the Age of Images, a Reason to Write Novels," *Harpers Magazine*, April 1996, reprinted as "Why Bother?," in Franzen, *How to Be Alone* (New York: HarperCollins, 2002), 77.

       There's the social isolate: Quoted in ibid.

171   *Reading serious literature impinges*: Quoted in ibid., 81.

173   *a mysterious force that everyone feels*: Federico García Lorca, "*Theory and Play of the Duende*" *and "Imagination, Inspiration, Evasion"* (Dallas: Kanathos, 1981), 61.

174   *All love songs must contain duende*: Nick Cave, *The Secret Life of the Love Song/ The Flesh Made Word* (London: Ellipses London, 2000), Audio-CD.

175   *Ring the bells*: Leonard Cohen, "Anthem," *The Future*, Columbia Records, 1992. As I was editing this page, I paused for a short break and read the news that Leonard Cohen had just died.

       Today we are seeing the birth: Jean Vanier, *The Broken Body: Journey to Wholeness* (London: Dartman, Longman & Todd, 1988), 11.

176   *O guiding dark of night!*: St. John of the Cross, *The Poems of St. John of the Cross*, trans. Kathleen Jones (London: Burns & Oats, 1993).

179   *But some recent research seeks*: See, for example, Megan Hustad, "The Surprising Benefits of a Tough Childhood," *Psychology Today*, March 2017, www.psychologytoday.com/articles/201703/the-surprising-benefits -tough-childhood. Or Willem E. Frankenhuis and Carolina de Weerth, "Does Early-Life Exposure to Stress Shape, or Impair, Cognition?," *Current Directions in Psychological Science* 22 (September 2013): 407-12.

IVP PRAXIS

EQUIPPING LEADERS FOR MINISTRY

"...TO EQUIP HIS PEOPLE FOR WORKS OF SERVICE,

SO THAT THE BODY OF CHRIST MAY BE BUILT UP."

EPHESIANS 4:12

God has called us to ministry. But it's not enough to have a vision for ministry if you don't have the practical skills for it. Nor is it enough to do the work of ministry if what you do is headed in the wrong direction. We need both vision *and* expertise for effective ministry. We need *praxis*.

Praxis puts theory into practice. It brings cutting-edge ministry expertise from visionary practitioners. You'll find sound biblical and theological foundations for ministry in the real world, with concrete examples for effective action and pastoral ministry. Praxis books are more than the "how to"—they're also the "why to." And because *being* is every bit as important as *doing*, Praxis attends to the inner life of the leader as well as the outer work of ministry. Feed your soul, and feed your ministry.

If you are called to ministry, you know you can't do it on your own. Let Praxis provide the companions you need to equip God's people for life in the kingdom.

www.ivpress.com/praxis